The Reach for Empire

By the Editors of Time-Life Books

Alexandria, Virginia

TIME
LIFE ®

Time-Life Books Inc.
is a wholly owned subsidiary of

Time Incorporated

Editor-in-Chief: Jason McManus
Chairman and Chief Executive Officer:
J. Richard Munro
President and Chief Operating Officer:
N. J. Nicholas, Jr.
Editorial Director: Richard B. Stolley

The Time Inc. Book Company

President and Chief Executive Officer:
Kelso F. Sutton
President, Time Inc. Books Direct:
Christopher T. Linen

Time-Life Books Inc.

EDITOR: George Constable
Executive Editor: Ellen Phillips
Director of Design: Louis Klein
Director of Editorial Resources: Phyllis K. Wise
Editorial Board: Russell B. Adams, Jr., Dale M.
Brown, Roberta Conlan, Thomas H. Flaherty, Lee
Hassig, Donia Ann Steele, Rosalind Stubenberg
Director of Photography and Research:
John Conrad Weiser
Assistant Director of Editorial Resources:
Elise Ritter Gibson

PRESIDENT: John M. Fahey, Jr.
Senior Vice Presidents: Robert M. DeSena,
James L. Mercer, Paul R. Stewart, Joseph J. Ward
Vice Presidents: Stephen L. Bair, Stephen L.
Goldstein, Juanita T. James, Andrew P. Kaplan,
Carol Kaplan, Susan J. Maruyama, Robert H.
Smith
Supervisor of Quality Control: James King

PUBLISHER: Joseph J. Ward

The Cover: A twin-engine Heinkel 111 rains
bombs on Warsaw in September 1939 during the
blitzkrieg that triggered World War II. After years
of enlarging the Reich through bullying and
diplomatic bluff, Hitler finally met in Poland an
opponent that chose to fight rather than yield.

This volume is one of a series that chronicles
the rise and eventual fall of Nazi Germany. Other
books in the series include:
The SS
Fists of Steel
Storming to Power
The New Order

The Third Reich

SERIES DIRECTOR: Thomas H. Flaherty
Series Administrator: Jane Edwin
Editorial Staff for *The Reach for Empire:*
Designer: Raymond Ripper
Picture Editor: Jane Coughran
Text Editors: Stephen G. Hyslop, John Newton,
Henry Woodhead
Researchers: Paula York-Soderlund (principal),
Karen Monks, Trudy Pearson
Assistant Designers: Alan Pitts, Tina Taylor
Copy Coordinator: Charles J. Hagner
Picture Coordinator: Robert H. Wooldridge, Jr.
Editorial Assistant: Patricia D. Whiteford

Special Contributors: Ronald H. Bailey, Lydia
Preston Hicks, Thomas A. Lewis, Mayo Mohs,
R. W. Murphy, David S. Thomson (text); Martha
Lee Beckington, Robin Currie, Oobie Gleysteen,
Marilyn Murphy (research); Michael Kalen Smith
(index)

Editorial Operations
Copy Chief: Diane Ullius
Production: Celia Beattie
Library: Louise D. Forstall

Correspondents: Elisabeth Kraèmer-Singh
(Bonn); Christine Lieberman (New York); Maria
Vincenza Aloisi (Paris); Ann Natanson (Rome).
Valuable assistance was also provided by: Judy
Aspinall, Lesley Coleman, Christine Hinze
(London); Elizabeth Brown (New York); Michal
Donath (Prague); Ann Wise (Rome); Traudl
Lessing (Vienna); Bogdan Turek (Warsaw).

First printing. Printed in U.S.A.

Published simultaneously in Canada.
School and library distribution by Silver Burdett
Company, Morristown, New Jersey 07960.

TIME-LIFE is a trademark of Time Incorporated
U.S.A.

**Library of Congress Cataloging in
Publication Data**
The Reach for empire / by the editors of
Time-Life Books.
    p.   cm. — (The Third Reich)
    Bibliography: p.
    Includes index.
    ISBN 0-8094-6958-8.
    ISBN 0-8094-6959-6 (lib. bdg.)
    1. World War, 1939-1945. 2. Germany—
History—1933-1945. I. Time-Life Books.
II. Series.
D743.R33 1989   940.53—dc19   88-36914

Other Publications:

AMERICAN COUNTRY
VOYAGE THROUGH THE UNIVERSE
THE TIME-LIFE GARDENER'S GUIDE
MYSTERIES OF THE UNKNOWN
TIME FRAME
FIX IT YOURSELF
FITNESS, HEALTH & NUTRITION
SUCCESSFUL PARENTING
HEALTHY HOME COOKING
UNDERSTANDING COMPUTERS
LIBRARY OF NATIONS
THE ENCHANTED WORLD
THE KODAK LIBRARY OF CREATIVE PHOTOG-
RAPHY
GREAT MEALS IN MINUTES
THE CIVIL WAR
PLANET EARTH
COLLECTOR'S LIBRARY OF THE CIVIL WAR
THE EPIC OF FLIGHT
THE GOOD COOK
WORLD WAR II
HOME REPAIR AND IMPROVEMENT
THE OLD WEST

For information on and a full description of any
of the Time-Life Books series listed above, please
call 1-800-621-7026 or write:
Reader Information
Time-Life Customer Service
P.O. Box C-32068
Richmond, Virginia 23261-2068

General Consultants

Col. John R. Elting, USA (Ret.), former associate professor at West Point, has written or
edited some twenty books, including *Swords
around a Throne, The Superstrategists,* and
American Army Life, as well as *Battles for
Scandinavia* in the Time-Life Books World
War II series. He was chief consultant to the
Time-Life series, The Civil War.

Gerhard L. Weinberg is a William Rand
Kenan, Jr., Professor of History at the University of North Carolina at Chapel Hill. He is
the author of *The Foreign Policy of Hitler's
Germany: Diplomatic Revolution in Europe,
1933-1936,* for which he received the George
Lewis Beer Prize of the American Historical
Association in 1971; *The Foreign Policy of
Hitler's Germany: Starting World War II,
1937-1939,* for which he received the Halverson Prize of the Western Association of German Studies in 1981; and other books and
articles. Professor Weinberg received a B.A.
degree from the State University of New York,
Albany, and M.A. and Ph.D. degrees from the
University of Chicago.

Contents

Berlin, April 20, 1939: A regimental band goose-steps past Hitler on his fiftieth birthday.

Motorized infantry units join the birthday parade down Berlin's majestic Unter den Linden.

Heavy, mechanized artillery lumbers past the Führer's reviewing stand.

A motorcycle reconnaissance squad exemplifies the German war machine, poised to fulfill Hitler's ambitions.

A Relentless Drive for Living Space

Four days after becoming chancellor of Germany, Adolf Hitler met with his senior generals at 14 Bendlerstrasse, the Berlin residence of Colonel General Kurt von Hammerstein-Equord, the commander in chief of the German army. The occasion, on February 3, 1933, was a dinner party to celebrate the sixtieth birthday of the foreign minister, Constantin von Neurath. Hitler's presence, however, provided Neurath and the military establishment with an unexpected opportunity to hear their new chancellor unbend in private.

For much of the evening, the former corporal seemed ill at ease among all the brass. The generals were the elite of Germany's grand military tradition, men whom Hitler both admired and distrusted, and he needed their help to rearm the Reich and consolidate his power. After the meal, however, Hitler took command. He rose, tapped a glass for silence, and addressed the leaders he hoped would one day execute his ambitious plans for the expansion of the Reich.

Hitler spoke for two hours, ranging across a number of topics. According to General Hammerstein's adjutant, who sat discreetly behind a curtain taking notes, Hitler labeled democracy the "worst of all possible evils." He promised to eradicate Marxism "root and branch," to restore German military might, and to "weld together" the nation—a task that "cannot be done by persuasion alone, but only by force."

At the heart of Hitler's rambling remarks was the concept of lebensraum, or living space. Germany, he insisted, needed "new lebensraum for our population surplus." One of the generals present quoted him as calling for the "conquest of new living space in the east and its ruthless Germanization." Here, for those who listened closely, was a blueprint of Hitler's plans for foreign adventure. He intended not merely to rebuild the armies of the Reich but to unleash them upon a series of countries: Austria, Czechoslovakia, Poland, and, one day, the Soviet Union. This, of course, meant war.

Several of the generals came away from the dinner party shocked and alarmed, although in fact Hitler had said nothing new. For nearly a decade, he had been saying publicly what he proclaimed privately that night. As

Members of the League of German Girls offer flowers to German cavalrymen entering Düsseldorf in March 1936. The troops were part of the 22,000-man force that Hitler ordered into the demilitarized Rhineland in defiance of the Treaty of Versailles and the Locarno Pact.

early as 1924, while in Landsberg prison, he had recorded his ideas on foreign policy in his book *Mein Kampf.* Some of his early goals coincided with the widely held views of conventional German nationalism. Hitler favored German union with his native Austria, for example, and he wanted to abrogate the Treaty of Versailles, through which the world war's victors had shrunk Germany's borders and severely limited German rearmament.

His aims, however, went much further. In *Mein Kampf* and later in his speeches, he spelled out his plans for a Reich so vast that it would become "lord of the earth" and "master of the world." He believed Germany's destiny would be determined by race and space. Racial purity, he was convinced, was the prime determinant of history, and the Germans belonged to the superior Nordic race. However, to survive and to propagate this genetic superiority, Germany needed more territory.

In Hitler's vision of racial purity, an enlarged Reich would absorb major European enclaves of German descent. This meant not only Anschluss, or union, with Austria—a goal defined in the first paragraph of *Mein Kampf*— but also the absorption of some three million people of German ancestry in the area of western Czechoslovakia known as the Sudetenland. Hitler also wanted to reclaim the German-speaking regions of Poland, which the Versailles treaty had restored as a nation at the expense of the Reich. Poland, whose corridor to the Baltic Sea separated East Prussia from the fatherland, was the object of enmity and scorn among Germans in general.

Beyond Poland, of course, lay the seemingly limitless reaches of Russia. In casting an acquisitive glance that far, he parted company with many nationalists during the 1920s, because the Weimar government's relations with the Soviet Union were so amicable the German army was permitted to operate secret training bases there. For Hitler, however, Russia's potential value to the Reich was too great to be ignored—"Destiny itself seems to point the way for us here." The vast Ukraine and the steppes farther east could more than fulfill the need he perceived for arable land. The Russian people, in Hitler's estimation, were beneath consideration. He believed the Slavs to be genetic inferiors, and he blamed the Bolshevik Revolution on his racial bête noire, the Jews.

What Hitler had in mind for these lands once they were conquered went beyond old-fashioned colonization. He foresaw settlers of pure German stock supplanting the natives, who would be expelled or exterminated. His model was the European conquest and occupation of North America.

The drive for living space also helped determine Hitler's attitude toward France. German-French history was a record of hostility, most recently in the world war and the imposition of the Versailles treaty. And France's geographical position on Germany's western flank threatened Hitler's am-

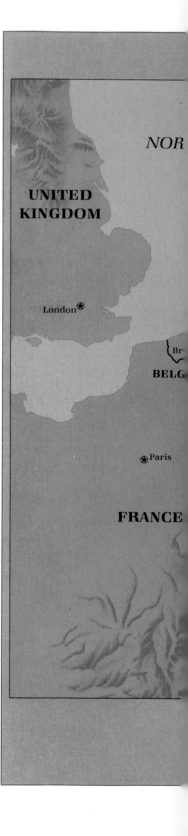

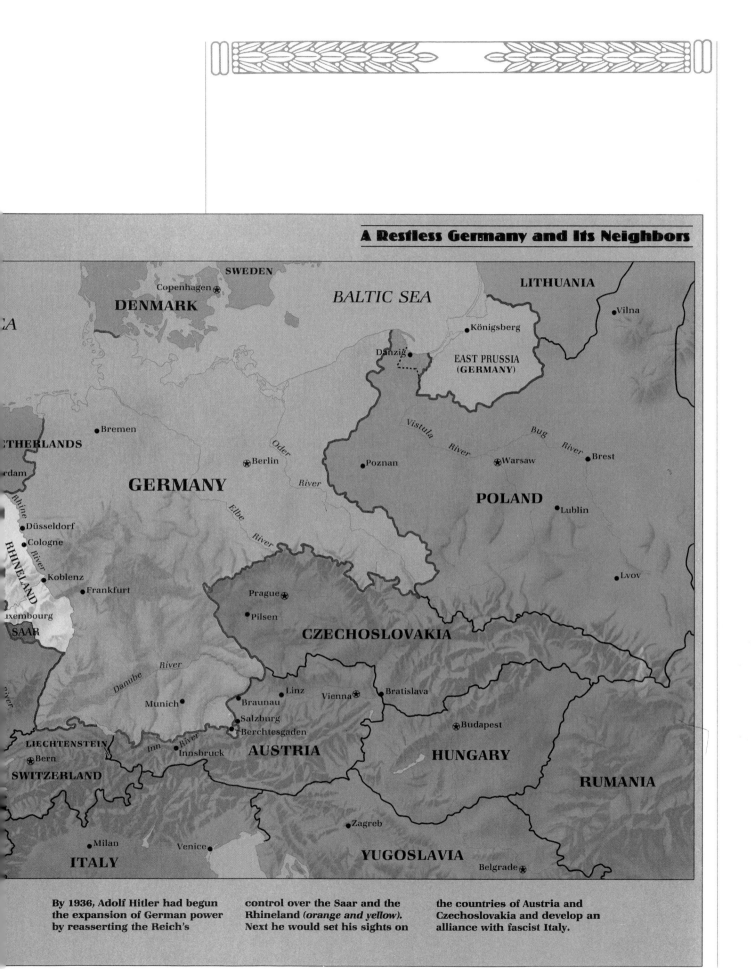

By 1936, Adolf Hitler had begun the expansion of German power by reasserting the Reich's control over the Saar and the Rhineland *(orange and yellow)*. Next he would set his sights on the countries of Austria and Czechoslovakia and develop an alliance with fascist Italy.

bitions in eastern Europe. The Führer reasoned that once he had committed his forces in a campaign to conquer the East, the French would surely attack him from the west. To avoid a two-front war, he would have to defeat France first.

For help against France, Hitler advocated the forging of alliances with two European powers that had opposed Germany during the Great War, Italy and Britain. He admired the Italian leader, Benito Mussolini, and saw the Fascist seizure of power there in 1922 as a portent of future Nazi success in Germany. Such an alliance made pragmatic as well as ideological sense in view of Italy's ambitions in the Mediterranean, which would clash with those of France. Hitler felt so strongly about cultivating Italy that he was willing to sacrifice claims to the South Tyrol, an Alpine region that Austria had lost to Italy in 1919.

As for the British, Hitler grudgingly admired them for what he saw as their inherent Nordic racial superiority. If the Führer succeeded in coming to terms with them, they might stand aside when Germany launched its campaign against the Soviet Union, whose communist government Britain abhorred. The Führer even believed that Great Britain might somehow be persuaded to help in his vaguely projected final stage of expansion, the conquest of the United States.

As chancellor, Hitler stuck to his original intentions but applied them flexibly. For example, he found it expedient to tone down his public comments on Germany's need to expand. By professing his desire for peace in his speeches, he pleased those at home and abroad who hoped for moderation. As his private remarks to the military establishment made clear, however, he had not changed his goals a whit. On February 8, five days after the dinner party at General Hammerstein's residence, Hitler told the German cabinet of his plans for full-scale rearmament: "The main principle must be: Everything for the armed forces!"

From the beginning, all of Hitler's policies—domestic as well as foreign—revolved around expansion. His first priority, solving the nation's economic crisis and putting people back to work, was necessary for the consolidation of his internal power. This consolidation would in turn provide the foundation for his foreign policy. And for Hitler, the role of foreign policy was not the traditional one of attaining objectives without war; rather, it was to put Germany in the best-possible position for actually waging war.

Hitler wanted to entrust the execution of foreign policy to a dependable loyalist. In 1931, he indicated that the post of foreign minister would go to Alfred Rosenberg, an all-purpose Nazi who performed such diverse jobs as editor of the party newspaper, *Völkischer Beobachter*, and leader of the

Fighting League for German Culture, an organization formed to combat modern tendencies in arts and letters. Rosenberg was a native of Estonia who had spent time in Moscow. These meager credentials qualified him as a foreign-affairs expert among the top Nazis, none of whom could claim much experience beyond the borders of Germany and Austria. But his appointment was thwarted by President Paul von Hindenburg, who insisted that his loyal associate, Neurath, be retained as foreign minister.

As a kind of consolation prize, Hitler created a foreign office within the Nazi party and appointed Rosenberg its chief. This agency, the Aussenpolitisches Amt, or APA, was structured much like the government's Foreign Office, and it was meant to be a springboard for a Nazi takeover of that conservative bastion. Rosenberg premiered in the international arena in May 1933, when Hitler sent him to London as his personal envoy to improve Nazi relations with the British government.

Ethnic German farmers in the Black Sea region of the Ukraine rest from stacking hay. Hitler's grand design called for reuniting such *Volksdeutsche* with the fatherland. He planned to kill or expel the vast majority of Ukrainians who were not ethnic Germans and make the area a giant breadbasket for the Reich.

The visit was a fiasco. Speaking no English and "palpably unacquainted with the British temperament," as the *Times* of London put it, he failed to impress British officials with his defense of the Nazis' persecution of the Jews and suppression of constitutional freedoms. He was snubbed by Prime Minister James Ramsay MacDonald and the Conservative party leader, Stanley Baldwin, who refused to see him. Rosenberg's mission reached its nadir when he laid a ceremonial wreath decorated with swastikas at the Cenotaph, the British war memorial. Members of an outraged British veterans' group denounced the wreath as a desecration and removed it the following day. The hapless emissary cut short his visit and returned home.

Two other cronies of Hitler turned out to be even larger embarrassments. Theodor Habicht was sent to Vienna as press attaché and chief Nazi watchdog in the German embassy. After only two weeks on the job, he was arrested for conspiring against the Austrian government. Robert Ley, the alcoholic chief of the German Labor Front, scandalized the International Workers' Conference in Geneva. Rejected as an official delegate to the conference, he blundered about drunkenly, loudly comparing the Latin American delegates to monkeys.

After such excesses, Hitler bowed to President Hindenburg's wishes and kept the veteran diplomat Neurath as foreign minister. The scion of Swabian aristocracy, son of a courtier to the king of Württemberg, Neurath had entered the imperial foreign service in 1901. He had served as envoy to Denmark, Italy, and Great Britain before his appointment to head the Foreign Office in 1932. A genial, frock-coated conservative, he preferred the life of the country gentleman to the duties of diplomacy. An ambassador recalled that Neurath "did not possess any great zeal for work." He loved to hunt, but in a leisurely fashion. Neurath "does not like to stalk game," a friend said. "He shoots it from his station."

Estonian-born Alfred Rosenberg *(left),* head of the Nazi party's foreign office, strolls along a London street with a colleague in May 1933. Rosenberg's efforts to win understanding for Hitler failed in England; one British official described him as a "Balt who looked like a cold cod."

Like many other old-line nationalists who thought they could somehow moderate Hitler's extreme views, Neurath cooperated with the Nazis after their rise to power in 1933. He privately expressed contempt for anti-Semitic rowdies and tried to protect several of his subordinates who were Jewish, yet he happily moved into a house expropriated from its Jewish owner. An American embassy official in Berlin shuddered at Neurath's "remarkable capacity for submitting to what in normal times could only be considered affronts and indignities on the part of the Nazis."

Practically all of the career diplomats serving under Neurath followed his lead and stayed on the job, determined "to make the best of the Nazis," as he put it. With rare exceptions—such as the German ambassador to the United States, Friedrich W. von Prittwitz und Gaffron, who resigned for reasons of conscience—they shared many of Hitler's foreign-policy goals as well as his anti-Semitism. Hitler and his colleagues, on the other hand, despised the diplomats because of their superior educations and social backgrounds. The Führer's right-hand man, Hermann Göring, joked: "What does a legation counselor do all day long? In the forenoon he sharpens pencils, and afternoons he goes out to tea somewhere."

Nonetheless, Hitler welcomed the aura of respectability that Neurath and the diplomatic corps provided. The Führer wanted to project an image of foreign policy as usual while Germany rearmed itself in secret. He feared that France or Poland—or perhaps both countries—might launch a war against Germany before the Reich was ready. "We cannot at the moment prosecute a war," the chief of the army's general staff, General Wilhelm Adam, wrote in March of 1933. "We must do everything to avoid it, even at the cost of a diplomatic defeat."

Such concern was understandable. France's army was substantially larger than that of Germany, which was limited to 100,000 men by the Versailles treaty. In addition, the treaty-enforced demilitarization of Germany's western border region, the Rhineland, left the Reich vulnerable to a French invasion. To the east, Poland possessed an army twice the size of Germany's and a strong current of nationalism to go with it. Soon after Hitler had come to power, in fact, Polish leader Józef Pilsudski discussed with his subordinates the possibility of occupying parts of Germany to make Hitler conform to the treaty's disarmament provisions. By some accounts, Pilsudski even sounded out the French about a joint attack on Germany, although nothing came of it.

The policy of rearming without provoking a preventive attack by its neighbors shaped German conduct at the Geneva disarmament conference, which was under way when Hitler became chancellor. Hitler detested German participation in these discussions as much as German membership in the League of Nations, which had been established as a peace-keeping forum after the world war. The talks could only lead to the kind of multilateral commitment he wanted to avoid. He much preferred bilateral agreements, which could be broken at will, without interference from a third party, when they no longer suited his purposes.

Hitler wanted to pull out of the disarmament discussions, so he protested publicly that the other powers were discriminating against Germany. He argued that if Germany were not allowed arms, it would remain vulnerable to attack. Either the Reich should be allowed to build up its forces for adequate self-defense or France and Britain should reduce their military strength to Germany's level. Hitler knew full well that the French were alarmed by the new Nazi regime and would refuse to make concessions. When the French stood firm as expected, he had his excuse. Asserting that Germany was being denied equal rights, he ordered his delegation in October 1933 to leave the conference. At the same time, he announced Germany's withdrawal from the League of Nations.

In order to bring home his bogus point about international injustice, Hitler staged a national plebiscite on his actions and won the backing of 95 percent of those voting. Neurath and other conservative diplomats approved as well. "We Germans were not suited to Geneva," wrote Ernst von Weizsäcker, a career diplomat and later the second-ranking official in the Foreign Office. "Our diplomats were unaccustomed to public addresses. The German, moreover, does not cut a happy figure at congresses. The chief beneficiaries of conferences, as far as I can see, are the representatives of dark-haired nations."

After abandoning the Geneva conference, Hitler continued his campaign of diplomatic duplicity, seeking to placate the neighbors he feared most while working behind the scenes to undermine their positions. He made a vigorous public appeal for friendship with France. At the same time, in January of 1934, he signed a ten-year nonaggression pact with Poland. Although the Foreign Office opposed the treaty, it was a coup for Hitler. The agreement made good propaganda, casting the Führer as a peaceable statesman. It also neutralized, at least for the time being, a potential threat to Germany from the east. And it drove a wedge between France and Poland, two countries that since 1921 had maintained an alliance aimed at containing Germany.

Hitler then tarnished his international image with a fiasco in Austria. In the hope of achieving Anschluss in one fell swoop, Hitler endorsed a coup attempt by Austrian Nazis in Vienna. The plotters assassinated the Austrian chancellor, Engelbert Dollfuss, on July 25, 1934, but they failed miserably to topple his government. News of the Dollfuss murder reverberated around the world. In New York, stock prices tumbled amid fears of a new war, and the *Times* of London commented that the killing "makes the name of Nazi stink in the nostrils of the world."

By 1935, Hitler had recovered from his embarrassment over the Dollfuss affair, and early that year he scored his first true international triumph. The Saar, a 1,000-square-mile border region rich in coal, had been taken from Germany in 1919 and placed under the auspices of the League of Nations. After fifteen years, the region's people were to choose their own allegiance. In a plebiscite on January 13, 1935, they voted overwhelmingly for reunion with the Reich. Hitler's victory was sweet: The valuable coal mines of the Saar River valley, given to France as compensation for damages caused to French coal fields during the Great War, now reverted to German control.

Thus encouraged, Hitler decided to unveil his rearmament program, which until now had been carried on by subterfuge. In March of 1935, two months after the Saar plebiscite, he announced the existence of the German air force, or Luftwaffe, and the introduction of general conscription. Both actions blatantly violated the Versailles settlement, but Hitler offered no excuses. Instead, he underscored his audacity by declaring that Germany would no longer observe the military limitations that had been imposed by the treaty.

Hitler's repudiation of Versailles stunned the European powers, which had mistakenly assumed that restoring the Saar to Germany would soften Hitler's stance, not toughen it. On April 11, the prime ministers of Britain, France, and Italy met in the little Italian town of Stresa to consider this new evidence of German belligerence. They agreed to stand together against any aggression by Germany, an alignment that was designated the Stresa Front. Three weeks later, the French succeeded in extending eastward the web of anti-German accords begun in Stresa. On May 2, France concluded a pact of mutual assistance with the Soviet Union. A fortnight later, the Soviet Union signed an affiliated agreement with Czechoslovakia.

Hitler, however, was engaged in diplomatic sleight of hand that threatened to crack the Stresa Front. Five months earlier, he had opened negotiations with the British over the size of the German navy. He proposed that if the British would ignore the Versailles treaty and recognize Germany's right to expand its navy, he would in return limit its size to one-third that of the Royal Navy. Such an agreement, Hitler reasoned, would reward the Reich in at least two ways: winning British approval of naval construction that was already well under way, and brewing trouble between Britain and France.

Hitler considered the negotiations with Great Britain so crucial that he

Coal miners in the Saar salute under a sign proclaiming, "We will vote for Germany on January 13"—a reference to the 1935 plebiscite to determine the future of their region.

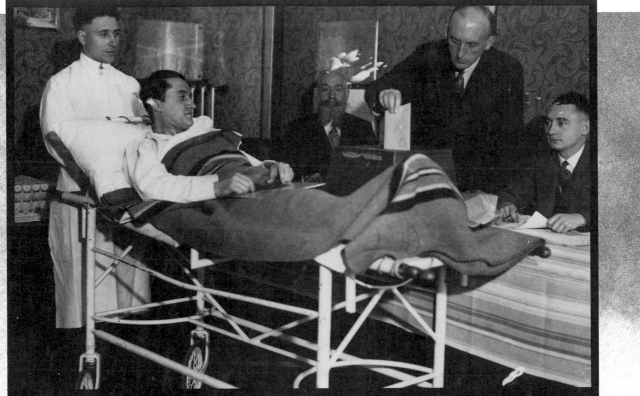

A hospital patient in the city of Saarbrücken has his ballot cast at a special booth set up in one of the wards. Of the more than 500,000 votes that were cast, 90 percent favored reunification with Germany.

Storm Troopers at the Feldherrnhalle in Munich celebrate the plebiscite results in front of an illuminated sign declaring, "The Saar is free."

himself took charge of the preliminary talks in Berlin. He was also growing impatient with Neurath and the hidebound procedures of the Foreign Office, which he referred to as an "intellectual garbage dump." When he asked the advice of diplomats, he complained, they always counseled doing nothing. Hitler told an underling that he had given the diplomats a good tongue-lashing: "I told those Father Christmases that what they were up to was good enough for quiet times, when they can all go their sleepy way, but not good enough for creating a new Reich."

In order to complete the delicate negotiations for a naval treaty with the British, Hitler called on Joachim von Ribbentrop, the forty-one-year-old former champagne salesman who had become his closest adviser on foreign affairs. Born in 1893 into modest circumstances—his father had been a lieutenant in the army artillery—Ribbentrop had established his own wine-and-spirits import business in Berlin after the world war and then married rich. His wife, Anneliese, was the socially prominent daughter of Otto Henkell, Germany's largest maker of champagne. Ribbentrop, adding luster to his new standing in society, acquired the title *von* by having himself adopted by a distant relative whose father had been knighted in the nineteenth century.

Ribbentrop joined the Nazi movement relatively late, becoming a member in May 1932. He quickly impressed Hitler, despite such liabilities as his monarchist sentiments and Jewish friends and business associates. With his cosmopolitan manner, command of French and English, and well-placed business contacts in Paris and London, Ribbentrop stood out from Hitler's parochial intimates. As Göring, with sarcasm but more than a trace of truth, put it, "Ribbentrop knows France through its champagne and England through its whiskey."

Hitler became a frequent guest at the Ribbentrop villa in a Berlin suburb. There the Führer learned appropriate table manners from Anneliese Ribbentrop, came to know the couple's upper-crust friends, and, in January 1933, conducted the secret negotiations that led to his selection as chancellor. He had Ribbentrop elected to the Reichstag and saw to his selection as a colonel in the Schutzstaffel (SS), the Führer's elite, black-shirted personal police force.

After Rosenberg's botched mission to London, Hitler gave Ribbentrop the go-ahead to set up yet another unofficial foreign ministry and to install himself as its chief. Known as the Ribbentrop Office and situated in a building directly across Wilhelmstrasse from the official Foreign Office, it attracted ambitious young men eager for a back door into the realm of diplomacy. Ribbentrop and his disciples, taking their orders directly from Hitler and cutting through the conventional red tape, successfully per-

Hitler's ambitious foreign-affairs adviser Joachim von Ribbentrop, whose wife Anneliese *(shown below with their child and pet)* was the daughter of a wealthy champagne producer, was reviled as an upstart by old-line Nazis. Said Joseph Goebbels, "Ribbentrop bought his name, he married his money, and he swindled his way into office."

formed several missions, including the inauguration of friendly contacts between German veterans' organizations and similar groups in Great Britain and France.

Even so, Ribbentrop was roundly disliked inside and outside of the Nazi party. He could be rude, overbearing, and superficial—a "husk with no kernel," sneered Franz von Papen, the aristocrat who served Hitler as vice chancellor and then as minister to Austria. Ribbentrop's crude approach to diplomacy was summed up in his suggestion that Winston Churchill, the staunch leader of the anti-Hitler faction in the British House of Commons, could be bought off with a bribe. Behind Ribbentrop's back, career diplomats derided him as a social climber, snickered at his clumsily written reports and indolent work habits, and confidently predicted that, like Alfred Rosenberg, he would trip up and fall from favor.

Ribbentrop's feuds with the Foreign Office, however, together with his unquestioning devotion, endeared him to Hitler. Ribbentrop was the "perfect courtier," according to André François-Poncet, who, as the French ambassador in Berlin, observed from a ringside seat. "He would hurl thunderbolts of flattery at Hitler without turning a hair," François-Poncet wrote. "His method of keeping in favor was very simple. It consisted of listening religiously to his master's endless monologues and in committing to memory the ideas developed by Hitler. Then, after Hitler had forgotten ever discussing them with Ribbentrop, the courtier passed them off as his own. Struck by this concordance, Hitler attributed to his collaborator a sureness of judgment and a trenchant foresight singularly in agreement with his own deepest thought."

Ribbentrop did not disappoint his Führer when negotiating the naval agreement with Great Britain in the spring of 1935. With characteristic obstinacy, he resisted British attempts to bring Germany back into the League of Nations as a precondition for the treaty. On June 18, without first consulting their Stresa Front partners, France and Italy, the British agreed to the Anglo-German Naval Agreement, limiting the German fleet to 35 percent of British tonnage.

The treaty was a coup for Ribbentrop and an even greater triumph for Hitler, who called June 18 the "happiest day of my life." In one stroke of the pen, he had both won from the British permission to rearm and cracked the solidarity of the Stresa Front. In a statement loaded with hypocrisy, he proclaimed that the naval pact was "only a preliminary to much wider cooperation" between what he called the "two great Germanic peoples."

Hitler's success with the British demonstrated his exceptional skill at sensing and exploiting the weaknesses of other nations. The British government did not lack sufficient warnings about the Nazis and their intentions. As early as 1933, the British ambassador in Berlin, Sir Horace Rumbold, had called attention to how closely the first three months of Hitler's government had followed the aggressive course set in *Mein Kampf.* And the British military delegate at the Geneva disarmament conference, Brigadier Arthur Temperley, reported bluntly, "There is a mad dog abroad once more, and we must resolutely combine to ensure either its destruction or at least its confinement until the disease has run its course." The British

Hitler listens intently to Sir John Simon, the British foreign secretary (*second from left*), during talks leading to the 1935 naval treaty that fixed German tonnage at 35 percent of the British fleet. Diplomat Anthony Eden (*on Simon's right*) said that Hitler ran the meeting "without hesitation and without notes, as befitted the man who knew where he wanted to go."

refused to face up to restraining the "mad dog" even after the formation of the Luftwaffe left their island dangerously open to air attack.

British timidity could be attributed only partly to the leadership of Prime Minister MacDonald and his successor, Baldwin. Revulsion against Continental entanglements ran deep among the British people. They were preoccupied with the economic havoc wrought by the depression: In 1933, Britain spent four times more on social services than on its armed forces. The British worried more about Japan's threat to the empire's Asian lifelines than about German submarines still on the drawing board, and Britain seemed content to have put an apparent lid on Hitler's naval rearmament. In addition, many Britons felt a lingering sense of guilt over Germany's supposedly harsh treatment under the Versailles settlement and did not begrudge Hitler what they saw as a modest increase in arms.

For their part, the French were dismayed by Hitler's aggressive maneuvering, but they were not ready to act against the Germans. Although they could field an army that was second in size only to the Soviet Union's, the French were divided by political and economic problems. The depression hit France later than most countries and stayed longer. Struggles between the Left and Right created political instability; the government changed twenty-four times during the 1930s, and morale suffered accordingly.

A few months after the Anglo-German Naval Agreement had opened a crack in French hopes for a united front against Germany, the prospect of unity began to crumble. Italy, driven by Mussolini's dreams of an African empire, invaded Ethiopia in October 1935. The duce had assumed that his partners in the Stresa Front would give him a free hand in Africa, but the invasion triggered conflict all around. The French, concerned more about German rearmament than about Mussolini's adventures in a far-off land, favored reconciliation with Italy. The British, responding to an upsurge of popular indignation at the use of European tanks and poison gas against primitive African weapons, demanded that the League of Nations impose economic sanctions against the aggressor. These demands turned out to be halfhearted, however, because Britain was unwilling to risk the war that might be ignited by strong sanctions. The desultory measures eventually taken were just enough to alienate Italy, spark disagreement between Britain and France, help cripple the League of Nations, and offer opportunity to Hitler—while failing utterly to solve the Ethiopian crisis.

Hitler seized upon the disarray among the Stresa powers to rearm the western frontier, a momentous step he had long contemplated. The Rhineland, as the region was known, covered 9,450 square miles of German territory west of the Rhine. It abutted Holland, Belgium, and France and encompassed Cologne and other major urban centers. The area, together

Citizens of Cologne welcome a column of German infantrymen marching across the Hohenzollern Bridge into the Rhineland on March 7, 1936. Eighteen years earlier, the defeated German army retreated from France across the same bridge.

A youngster pins a corsage on one of the soldiers who re-occupied Cologne. In order to achieve maximum coverage of such happy scenes, Propaganda Minister Goebbels had selected members of the German press flown in on a special plane.

with a strip extending thirty miles east of the river, had been demilitarized at Versailles in order to create a buffer zone between Germany and its western neighbors. Later, Germany had promised to respect the permanent demilitarization of the Rhineland by signing the Locarno Pact of 1925. This provision was generally considered to be the most important guarantee of peace in Europe. By sealing off the obvious staging area for an attack, it prevented a surprise German invasion of France or the Low Countries. At the same time, the role of Great Britain and Italy as guarantors of the Locarno Pact protected Germany against any armed reaction by the French.

Hitler realized that by marching into the Rhineland he risked triggering a full-scale war. But he shrewdly calculated the odds. Italy would not intervene, since Hitler already had Mussolini's assurances that he would ignore his obligations under the Locarno Pact. Britain was not likely to interfere on the Continent unilaterally, and France had shown a paralysis of will in the Ethiopian crisis. Hitler was gambling that France, with its internal divisions and imminent elections, could not summon the nerve to counter his move with force.

All the same, the military operation that Hitler launched on the morning of March 7, 1936, was carefully tailored to minimize provocation. Of the approximately 22,000 troops who marched into the demilitarized zone on the east bank, only about one-tenth continued westward across the bridges into the Rhineland proper. As they goose-stepped into Cologne and other cities to the cheers of flower-throwing crowds, Hitler unleashed a propaganda blitz. The blame, he declared, belonged to France. He said the French parliament had broken the Locarno Pact and upset the balance of power the previous month by formally ratifying its 1935 treaty with the Soviet Union. Despite that, Hitler continued, he was now offering the olive branch of peace. He stood ready to negotiate nonaggression pacts with France and Belgium, to discuss mutual limitations on air power, and even to engineer the return of Germany to the League of Nations. His sincerity could be measured by his gratuitous proposal to demilitarize both sides of Germany's border with France, a suggestion that would require the French to abandon the Maginot Line, their main defense against a German invasion.

Waiting for the reaction to his move, Hitler endured what he described later as the "most nerve-racking" forty-eight hours of his life. He need not have worried. The French government seemed paralyzed. No one in Paris had formulated a plan to counter the military occupation of the Rhineland, even though for months Ambassador François-Poncet had been warning of just such an occurrence. The government roused itself to move troops into the fortifications of the Maginot Line but did nothing more except condemn the Germans and take the matter before the League of Nations, which had already been discredited by its failure to intervene in Ethiopia. French military leaders wildly overestimated the strength of the German army and concluded—wrongly—that full-scale mobilization would be necessary to push the occupation force out of the Rhineland. They feared that the public was not prepared to support such a buildup.

Great Britain, while deploring Germany's breach of international order, seemed more concerned about preventing the French from doing anything about it. The British, who had led the argument for sanctions after Italian aggression in Ethiopia, now became the first to advise the French against imposing penalties on Germany. The cabinet had already decided before the occupation that the Rhineland was not a vital British interest. After all, intoned the *Times* of London, the Rhineland was German territory; Hitler was only "going into his own back garden."

Thus the Führer won his boldest gamble yet. By removing the possibility of a surprise French attack through the Rhineland, and by installing the Wehrmacht on the very frontier of Germany's old foe, he had shifted the

Hitler and his aides listen anxiously to radio reports of the reoccupation of the Rhineland. "If I had been the French," Hitler confided later, "I would not have allowed a single German soldier to cross the Rhine."

balance of power in western Europe. He had done it, moreover, with the acquiescence of the international community and despite the worried protests of his generals—factors that would profoundly shape his future policies. His people applauded; in a plebiscite on the Rhineland issue, 99 percent of the Germans who cast ballots approved. And his confidence soared. Increasingly, he would rely on his own judgment and worry less about the responses of his generals and the rest of the world.

After showing the iron fist so effectively, Hitler renewed his vigorous campaign to manipulate his Continental adversaries. In July 1936, he appointed Ribbentrop ambassador to London. There Ribbentrop preached the dangers of Soviet bolshevism. He portrayed Nazi Germany as the strongest bastion of anticommunism, an argument that appealed to many upper-class conservatives. But Ribbentrop was prone to gaffes, such as greeting the king with a Nazi salute at a court reception, and he gradually lost favor. Ribbentrop responded by cultivating a growing distaste for the British; he formed the conviction, which he expressed to Hitler, that they were "our most dangerous opponent."

Meanwhile, he devoted much of his time to wooing Japan, another object of the Führer's international courtship. Ribbentrop foresaw the advantages of better relations with the Asian power, which was already making mischief in China, and he persuaded Hitler to agree to a treaty with Japan over the objections of the Foreign Office. The resulting Anti-Comintern Pact of November 1936 did not amount to much in itself. It merely pledged Germany and Japan to "work in common against Communist disruptive influences"—namely, the Communist International, or Comintern, Moscow's instrument for controlling the foreign branches of the party. But the pact represented a first step toward the formation of an alliance that would soon threaten the peace on two continents.

The nation that would become the third member of that alliance, Italy, was the main object of Hitler's affections. The Führer had long felt a personal and ideological affinity with Mussolini. "This great man south of the Alps," as Hitler described the duce in *Mein Kampf*, had risen from humble birth, served as an army corporal during the Great War, and emerged to blaze the trail of fascism. To Hitler's dismay, however, Mussolini at first had not reciprocated the admiration. The Italian dictator dismissed Hitler's ideas as "little more than commonplace clichés" and described *Mein Kampf* as a "boring tome that I have never been able to read."

What bothered Mussolini most was Hitler's oft-stated goal of union between Germany and Austria. On Italy's northeastern frontier, the duce preferred a weak Austria to the prospect of an aggressive, German-

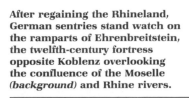

After regaining the Rhineland, German sentries stand watch on the ramparts of Ehrenbreitstein, the twelfth-century fortress opposite Koblenz overlooking the confluence of the Moselle *(background)* and Rhine rivers.

dominated one. Hitler had made his first trip abroad as chancellor, traveling to Venice in June 1934, largely to calm Mussolini's fears about Austria.

The meeting between the two strongmen went badly from the start. Mussolini arrived in full uniform and upstaged Hitler, who looked like a shabby salesman in his raincoat, soft hat, and patent-leather shoes. Hitler then monopolized the conversation. "He was a gramophone with just seven tunes," Mussolini complained, "and once he had finished playing them he started all over again." Another participant in the talks, the German foreign minister, Neurath, recalled that "their minds didn't meet; they didn't understand each other."

Understanding was severely handicapped by Mussolini's proud refusal to have an interpreter present to unravel Hitler's rapid-fire German. Indeed, the failure of communication might have resulted in Hitler's mistaken impression that Mussolini had lost interest in Austria and had even agreed to the installation of a pro-Nazi government in Vienna. Scarcely more than a month after the meeting came the Hitler-endorsed assassination of the Austrian chancellor, Dollfuss, an act that enraged Mussolini and put him at odds with the Germans.

During the next two years, however, events gradually conspired to drive Mussolini into Hitler's camp. First, Britain and France's negative reaction to his invasion of Ethiopia estranged Mussolini from his partners in the Stresa Front; in contrast, the Germans proclaimed neutrality and sold him coal and weapons. Then, Mussolini was so impressed by Hitler's unopposed occupation of the Rhineland that he backed away from his self-appointed role as Austria's protector and urged his neighbor to negotiate a pact with Germany. In the resulting agreement, signed on July 11, 1936, Hitler professed respect for Austrian independence and renounced his old policy of annexation. Finally, during that summer of 1936, Mussolini and Hitler found themselves fighting as allies on the same front. Both sent arms and troops to the Spanish Civil War to aid the Nationalist revolt of General Francisco Franco against the Republican government.

The amity between the two nations grew stronger. In October 1936, Mussolini's son-in-law and newly appointed foreign minister, Galeazzo Ciano, visited the Reich to conclude a secret agreement with Hitler that spelled out the two nations' common political and economic interests. The agreement was signed on October 23, the same day Ribbentrop completed negotiations with the Japanese on the Anti-Comintern Pact.

In Ciano's company, Hitler praised the duce as the "leading statesman in the world, to whom no one may even remotely compare himself." Mussolini responded a week later by referring publicly for the first time to a "vertical line between Rome and Berlin" around which Europe revolved.

He termed it an axis. This name for the new relationship between Germany and Italy would stick, and would later encompass a third partner, Japan.

While forging an alliance with Italy, Germany was emerging as the most powerful nation in Europe. Small countries feared the Reich, and powers such as Britain, France, and the Soviet Union grew increasingly uncertain about their relations with the new Germany. Hitler's intervention in the Spanish Civil War was paying dividends in addition to closer ties with Italy: The Reich's resurgent armed forces were rehearsing thousands of soldiers and testing new machines, badly needed minerals were flowing into Germany from Spanish mines, and Hitler was making useful anticommunist propaganda of the fight against the Soviet-aided Spanish Republicans.

German involvement in Spain signified another increment in the widening rift between Hitler and his official Foreign Office. Neurath had objected to intervention in Spain, and the Führer had ignored him. The hapless minister frequently complained of Hitler's failure to listen to him: "I am called upon to give advice and then not given a chance to say a word!" But on one issue the aristocratic Neurath remained stubbornly his own man. He refused to abide the proposed appointment of Ribbentrop as state secretary, the second-ranking job in the Foreign Office. Instead, he named his son-in-law, Hans Georg von Mackensen, a Nazi party member in good standing and the son of a retired field marshal. This apparent act of nepotism prompted the French ambassador, François-Poncet, to quip one day after leaving the Foreign Office, "I have seen the Father and the Son, but where is the Holy Ghost?"

To add steel to his armory for future foreign adventures, Hitler accelerated his rearmament drive by inaugurating the Four-Year Plan. This scheme, launched in October 1936, was intended to prepare Germany for war in four years. The war Hitler envisioned was not a single massive conflict but blitzkrieg, or lightning warfare—a series of quick and decisive conquests. The Four-Year Plan aimed at reducing the Reich's dependency on imports by expanding the production of synthetic oil and rubber and making use of low-grade domestic iron ore. These measures would pave the way for the tanks and planes of blitzkrieg. Hermann Göring headed the Four-Year Plan as well as the Luftwaffe. "We are already at war," he told his generals in December 1936. "Only the shooting has not yet started."

The shooting drew closer with every weapon that rolled off the assembly line, yet Hitler's top commanders seemed cautious. Despite their knowledge of the Four-Year Plan, and despite their Führer's bellicose pronouncements, the generals failed to concede the inevitability of war. Hitler railed impatiently at their hesitancy and lack of passion. In an effort to impress

Foreign Minister Galeazzo Ciano of Italy is flanked by his German counterpart Constantin von Neurath *(right)* **and Hermann Göring at the 1936 meeting in Berlin where Ciano signed a secret protocol defining the two nations' common interests.**

them with the imminence of the conflict and to kindle their enthusiasm, he convened a meeting in the Reich Chancellery on November 5, 1937. Göring was there, along with Foreign Minister Neurath and Field Marshal Werner von Blomberg, the minister of war; also in attendance were Colonel General Werner von Fritsch, commander in chief of the army, and Admiral Erich Raeder, head of the navy. Ostensibly, the meeting had been called in order to air a bitter policy dispute between Blomberg and Göring, who was using his position as director of the Four-Year Plan to favor the Luftwaffe in the allocation of steel and other scarce raw materials. But the real purpose of the meeting, as Hitler later described it, was "to put some steam up the pants" of the generals.

The meeting lasted for more than four hours, and much of the discussion was committed to paper by Hitler's conscientious military adjutant, Colonel Friedrich Hossbach. According to Hossbach's notes, Hitler announced that what he had to say was so important he wanted it regarded as "his last will and testament" in the event of his death. Hitler was only forty-eight years old, but he had been deeply affected by his mother's death from cancer and was obsessed with the notion that he might die before Germany achieved its destiny.

Having sounded that morbid note, Hitler launched into a subject that had dominated his first meeting with the generals soon after he had come to power: the desperate need for lebensraum, or living space. Germany's very future, he said, depended upon lebensraum for growing sufficient food and obtaining raw materials, such as copper and tin, that were not available within the Reich's present territory. International trade was no solution, because it limited Germany's independence and led to "pronounced military weakness." Nor did Hitler dream of overseas ex-

Bulwark on the Western Front

One of Hitler's first moves after re-militarizing the Rhineland was to build the West Wall, a band of fortifications intended to protect Germany's western frontier. The wall began modestly with a series of small forts along the Saar River opposite the Maginot Line. But in 1938, as Hitler looked covetously at Czechoslovakia, the project took on new importance. The Führer ordered the defenses extended from Holland in the north to the Swiss border in the south.

Under Fritz Todt, the engineer who built the autobahn, half a million laborers worked twelve-hour days building bunkers, pillboxes, and antitank barriers. Simultaneously, the Nazis disseminated propaganda to convince the world that the West Wall had changed the strategic map of Europe. "As soon as our fortifications are constructed and the countries of central Europe realize that France cannot enter German territory at will," a Nazi official explained, "they will begin to feel very differently about their foreign policies, and a new constellation will develop."

An illustration of a West Wall bunker from a contemporary magazine portrays a giant complex many stories deep. Although the actual bunkers were not so elaborate, they did contain command posts, troop quarters, and ammunition-storage areas.

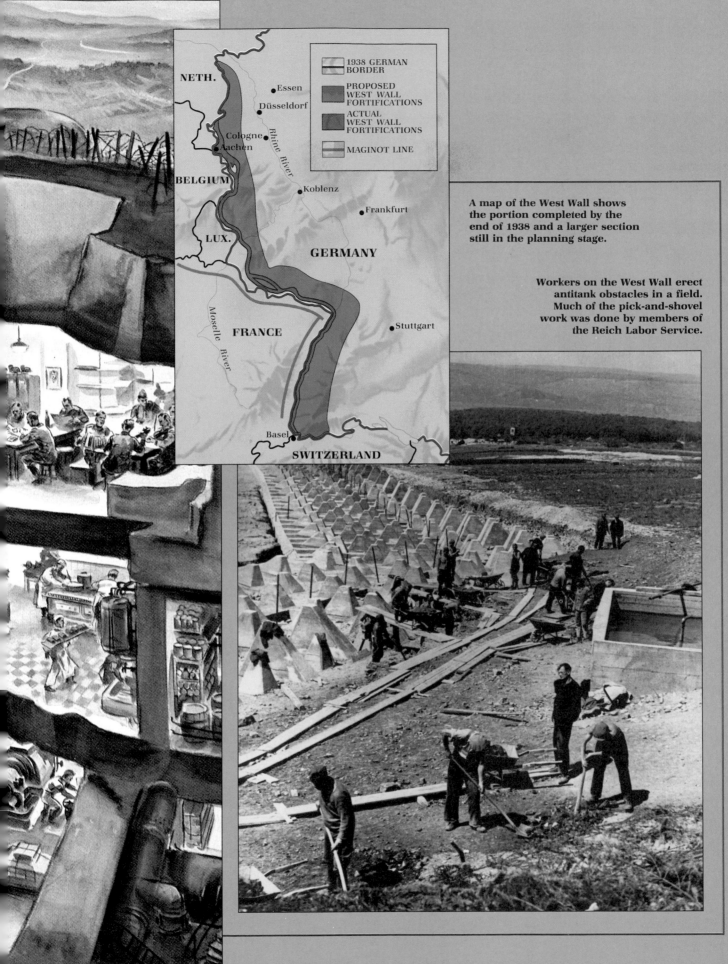

Map legend

- 1938 GERMAN BORDER
- PROPOSED WEST WALL FORTIFICATIONS
- ACTUAL WEST WALL FORTIFICATIONS
- MAGINOT LINE

NETH.

Essen

Düsseldorf

Cologne
Aachen

Rhine River

BELGIUM

Koblenz

LUX.

Frankfurt

GERMANY

Moselle River

FRANCE

Stuttgart

Basel

SWITZERLAND

A map of the West Wall shows the portion completed by the end of 1938 and a larger section still in the planning stage.

Workers on the West Wall erect antitank obstacles in a field. Much of the pick-and-shovel work was done by members of the Reich Labor Service.

pansion. Lebensraum, he continued, should be pursued by the annexation of regions near the Reich—and "could be solved only by the use of force."

Hitler branded Britain and France as Germany's main adversaries—"two hate-inspired antagonists." He was confident that the British, for the time being, at least, would not use force to stop German expansion. The British empire was in the process of dissolution, and Britons in general loathed the prospect of entanglement in another protracted European war. Hitler also expressed doubt that the French would pursue "warlike action against Germany." Nonetheless, the Reich must move against the West before 1943. By then, he predicted, France and Great Britain would wake up and arm to meet the German challenge.

As his first targets for takeover, Hitler singled out Austria and Czechoslovakia. Control over these two countries not only would buffer Germany's southeastern flank but would add tens of thousands of fresh soldiers for ventures to come. Hitler asserted that swift action toward these objectives would forestall any armed response by Poland and the Soviet Union. France might be diverted by the eruption of internal disorders or even by a war with Italy arising from tensions in Spain. If so, Hitler said, the opportunity to move against Austria and Czechoslovakia might come "as early as 1938"—the following year.

Hitler had said much of this before, but never with such dramatic immediacy. Faced with the prospect of waging war within a few months, Blomberg and Fritsch hoisted warning flags. They did not object in principle to the annexation of Austria and Czechoslovakia but hesitated to risk a full-scale war. They counseled Hitler against making enemies of Britain and France and expressed concern about the Reich's readiness to fight.

When discussion turned to the meeting's original agenda—Göring's biased allocations of raw materials—Blomberg and Fritsch complained so vehemently that Hitler's face registered surprise and dismay. Colonel Hossbach later concluded that their conduct throughout the meeting "must have made plain to Hitler that his policies had met with objective opposition, not approval and compliance."

This demonstration of independent thinking by two of his top officers disturbed Hitler. At such moments, Blomberg and Fritsch—both of whom had been appointed by the late President Hindenburg—typified the Prussian aristocratic military tradition, with its rigid conservatism, that Hitler secretly detested. But these two officers were in truth often at loggerheads with each other. Blomberg, sixty years old, was tall, thin, and sociable, and he had proved to be one of Hitler's most compliant allies in the armed forces. He was so slavish in his devotion to the Führer that many in the

Paratroopers drop from the sky and Panzer I tanks roll across a field during a mock battle outside Hameln in October 1936. The military demonstration was staged for the tens of thousands of spectators attending the annual Nazi harvest festival.

officer corps referred to him as the Rubber Lion. By contrast, Fritsch was considered a model of probity by his subordinates. At the age of fifty-eight, he stood ramrod straight and was just as unbending in his quiet distaste for Hitler. "I wear a monocle," he once remarked, "so that my face remains stiff when I confront that man."

Their differences aside, both of the officers were too cautious for Hitler. The meeting was not the first time they had shown a lack of verve and determination. They consistently dragged their feet in expanding the armed forces, he felt, and both had advised him against occupation of the Rhineland in 1936. Hitler's boldness had won the day there, and as his power and self-confidence grew, he felt increasing contempt for the generals and other conservatives and less need to court them. Now that he was ready to raise the pressure on Germany's neighbors, Hitler wanted unquestioning subordinates who were prepared to execute his aggressive policies with zeal and dispatch.

A man more eager than even Hitler to get rid of Blomberg and Fritsch afforded an opportunity to shake up the high command. Göring smarted from their barbs about his direction of the Four-Year Plan, but he had more than revenge in mind. The Luftwaffe chief wanted Blomberg's job as minister of war so that he could command not merely the air force but the entire Wehrmacht. In pursuit of that goal, Göring set about orchestrating not one but two sensational sex scandals.

Blomberg was the first victim. A widower, he fell in love with a young working woman named Erna Gruhn and married her on January 12, 1938. Even though Göring possessed shocking information about Gruhn given him by the Berlin police, he and the Führer himself served as witnesses at the modest wedding ceremony in the War Ministry. Unknown to the aristocratic Blomberg, who thought he had married a "child of the people," as he told Hitler, Gruhn had posed for pornographic pictures and had a criminal record for prostitution. When Göring revealed this to Hitler twelve days after the wedding, the Führer, who never paid attention to the personal affairs of his Nazi confederates, now professed incredulity. "If a German field marshal will marry a whore," he muttered, "then anything can happen in the world."

Göring confronted the war minister with the lurid information, and Blomberg, stunned, voluntarily resigned. Göring turned immediately to the matter of Fritsch, who, as army commander, was the logical successor to Blomberg. A bachelor not known to consort with women, Fritsch presented a different kind of target. With the connivance of Heinrich Himmler, chief of the SS and the Gestapo, Göring dredged up old charges by a male prostitute that an army officer named Fritsch had engaged in homosexual

Vacationing in Ceylon in May 1938, sixty-year-old Field Marshal Werner von Blomberg walks with his twenty-five-year-old bride, Erna. Her past as a prostitute and pornography model gave the Nazi government grounds to destroy Blomberg's career.

acts. Although Göring knew that the officer in question was actually a retired cavalry captain named Frisch (the name was even spelled differently), he framed the general. Fritsch demanded a court-martial and was eventually exonerated, but too late. Hitler, despite knowing of Göring's deception, had already acted to remove Fritsch from command.

On February 4, the Führer announced the resignations of Blomberg and Fritsch "for reasons of health." To succeed Fritsch as commander in chief of the army, Hitler selected Colonel General Walther von Brauchitsch, a competent but compliant descendant of a Prussian military family. Brauchitsch readily agreed to Hitler's stipulation that he retire sixteen senior generals and transfer forty-four others. The new commander's own personal problems helped ensure his loyalty to the Führer. By promising to provide 80,000 marks, or 20,000 dollars, to Brauchitsch so that he could settle a divorce with his long-estranged wife, Hitler enabled the general to marry his mistress. From time to time, the Führer would allude to this financial arrangement in the presence of Brauchitsch and fellow officers; the army commander was so intimidated, according to his chief of staff, that he would stand numbly before Hitler "like a little cadet before his commandant."

Hitler's announcement brought other surprises. Göring was promoted to field marshal but not to succeed Blomberg. That honor fell to Hitler, who abolished the position of war minister and named himself commander in chief of the armed forces. At the same time, Hitler retired his cautious sixty-five-year-old foreign minister, Neurath, whose agitation at the Führer's bellicose intentions had triggered a recent series of heart seizures. Hitler replaced him with the sycophantic Ribbentrop, who quickly substituted military uniforms for the customary frock coat and striped pants worn by his diplomats and marched his deputies Nazi-style about the courtyard of their Wilhelmstrasse headquarters.

Ever the opportunist, Hitler had seized the chance to break the old aristocracy's hold on both the army and the Foreign Office and assume control. Almost five years to the day after first meeting with his conservative paladins of national security, he was rid of their restraint and ready to unleash the reborn power of the Third Reich. ✚

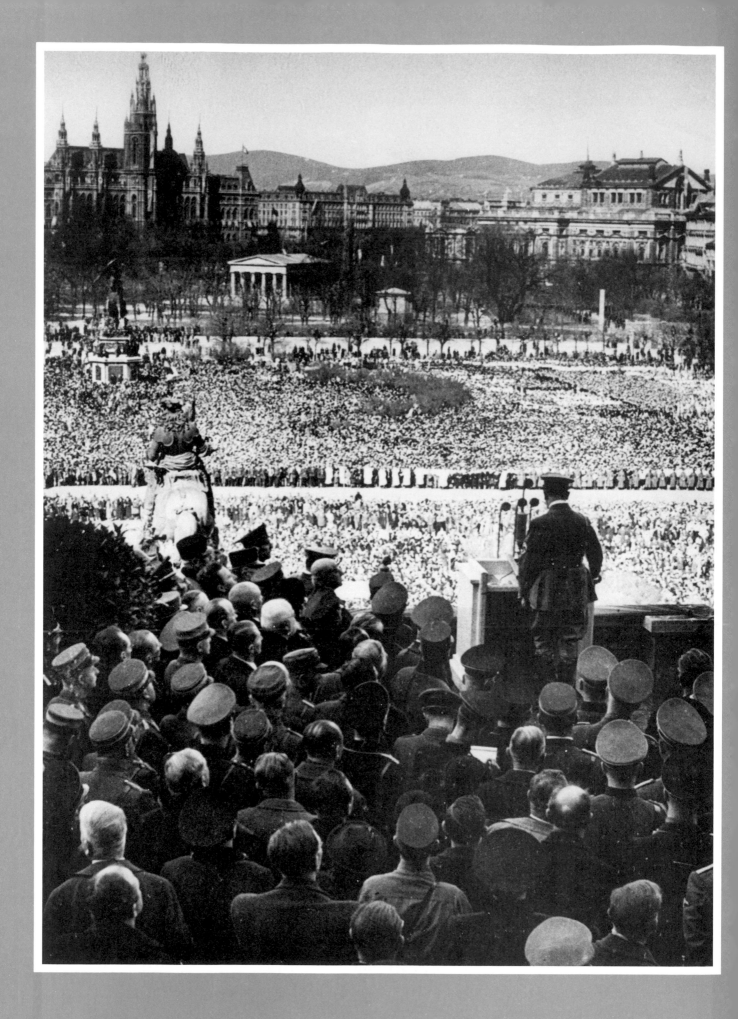

TWO

"One Blood, One Reich"

ess than three weeks from Ash Wednesday, when the gray curtain of Lent would lower on Vienna's glittering social life, the Viennese were waltzing away the evenings before the season of penance began. On Friday night, February 11, 1938, the focus of the festivities was a ball sponsored by the Fatherland Front, the dominant force in Austria's authoritarian state.

Kurt von Schuschnigg, chancellor of Austria and leader of the Fatherland Front, dressed for the occasion in his dark blue uniform as chief of the Sturmkorps, a paramilitary elite that had been created to defend Schuschnigg's regime against its militant opponents. A crusader-like cross, the emblem of the Fatherland Front, gleamed from lapels and flew from banners around the festive hall. Nothing in the outward manner of the chancellor or his guests hinted that this was to be the last hurrah for the front, or that Austria's time of penance would last not for weeks, but for seven arduous years.

As he played the gracious host, however, Schuschnigg was steeling himself for the sternest test of his tenure, a confrontation so risky he insisted on keeping it secret. The next morning, he would come face to face with Adolf Hitler in the Berghof, the Führer's Alpine retreat, which perched so close to the frontier it commanded a view of the Austrian city of Salzburg.

Shortly before midnight, Schuschnigg and his foreign minister, Guido Schmidt, left the ball, ostensibly to catch the night train to Innsbruck for a relaxing weekend in the Tyrol. They boarded the train with their skis. But once they reached Salzburg, their car was detached and moved to a siding, where the two men awaited their morning ride to the Berghof.

Hitler and Schuschnigg shared a concern that would dominate the Berghof meeting, the idea of Anschluss, or union—the union of Austria with the Third Reich, the marriage of one German-speaking state with another, of the ancient imperial capital of Vienna with the new Reich capital of Berlin. Schuschnigg knew that the Nazis regarded the union as inevitable, and he came to the Berghof to resist it, to plead for a renewal of Germany's 1936 pledge to honor Austrian independence. He was ready to offer concessions to Hitler if they would end the hostile maneuvers of

Speaking on March 15, 1938, from the balcony of the Hofburg, former seat of the Habsburg emperors in Vienna, Hitler proclaims the entry of Austria into the Third Reich. The union climaxed a relentless campaign by Hitler and his Austrian partisans to undermine the independence of the country.

the outlawed Austrian Nazi party—including a coup attempt that had been uncovered in Vienna only a month before.

Hitler had trumpeted his intentions for Austria fourteen years earlier in the opening words of *Mein Kampf.* His birth at Braunau, just inside the Austrian border, was providential, he wrote: "This little town lies on the boundary of two German states that we of the younger generation, at least, have made it our lifework to reunite by every means at our disposal. German Austria must return to the great German mother country. One blood demands one Reich." Far from acknowledging any responsibility to restrain his supporters in Austria, Hitler planned to press Schuschnigg to restore Nazis to positions of authority and so hasten the day when Vienna would march to Berlin's tune. Hitler knew that a diplomatic victory over Austria would also serve his interests at home by distracting those who were unsettled by his recent purge of conservatives in the army and Foreign Office and resisted his aggressive ambitions.

There was, however, far more to the argument between Hitler and Schuschnigg than one's ambition and the other's resistance. The agenda each man carried into the arena was freighted with hundreds of years of history, centuries in which their two lands had engaged in a fitful courtship marked by violent quarrels and fervent attempts at reconciliation. As both leaders knew, the time for a free and amicable union was past. It was still to be seen whether the relationship between their states would remain one of estrangement or whether, as recent events suggested, the epic affair would end in a last, devouring embrace.

For the Nazis, the idea of Anschluss had deep historical roots. The lands that would later be known as Germany and Austria had been united under the First Reich—the Holy Roman Empire established in the tenth century by the German king, Otto I, who claimed the mantle of the Frankish conqueror, Charlemagne. Otto's domain covered much of Europe—from the Baltic Sea through the Alpine region and Danube basin south to central Italy. Some regarded this as a precedent for Hitler's territorial ambitions. But this First Reich, which Nazi ideologues looked to so proudly, was a troubled house built on a weak foundation. The papacy and princes of the realm often challenged Otto's heirs. It fell to Austria's ruling family, the Habsburgs—who inherited the vestiges of the empire in the fifteenth century—to restore and expand it through a succession of marriage alliances. In the process, the Habsburg capital of Vienna, once a bleak Roman outpost harried by barbarians, grew to rival Paris in culture and refinement.

The Habsburgs themselves were not always masters of their domain. During the Reformation, they kept their subjects in Austria and Hungary faithful to the Roman church but were opposed by German Protestants—evidence that the ties of language and custom that linked Germany to Vienna were fragile indeed. In the eighteenth century, German defiance of the Habsburgs coalesced in Prussia, whose leaders proclaimed themselves kings, entitled to negotiate as equals with Austria's rulers. Although the two powers joined forces against Napoléon and remained allied once that threat was removed in 1814, Prussia's ambitions were to collide with Austria's imperial claims. The showdown came in 1866, when Prussia, in league with a recently unified Italy, won a seven-week war against Austria and its German dependents, including Hanover and Bavaria. The victory led to the emergence of a muscular Prusso-German Empire—the Second Reich that Hitler regarded as the immediate precedent for his Nazi state.

Overshadowed now by Berlin, Vienna struggled to adjust to its reduced circumstances. In 1867, the Habsburg realm was officially reconstituted as Austria-Hungary, a concession that appeased the restive Hungarians but did nothing to satisfy the empire's other defiant ethnic groups, notably the Czechs and the Serbs. German language and culture remained dominant in and around Vienna, but the German Austrians felt besieged by their minorities and no longer certain of their identity.

In some quarters of the capital, the glow of the imperial sunset diverted attention from the deepening fissures. The Vienna of the late nineteenth century was a place of creative ferment—home to psychoanalyst Sigmund Freud, painter Gustav Klimt, composers Gustav Mahler and Johann Strauss. The theaters and cafés had never been more crowded, the talk of art and ideas never more fevered. Yet some ideas were poisonous, and the toxins would surface with astonishing virulence in the next century.

Stung by Austria's defeat in 1866, young German Austrians looked to the victor for leadership. They adopted pan-Germanism, a vision of a greater Reich linking the predominantly German regions of Austria-Hungary to the kaiser's Germany. The idea enthralled one young Austrian who moved to the capital in 1907. "When I came to Vienna," Hitler recalled in *Mein Kampf*, "my sympathies were fully and wholly on the side of the pan-German tendency." The demagogue Georg von Schönerer, a rich landowner, rallied Hitler and other Austrians to this cause. Schönerer sweetened his pan-Germanism with demands for workers' rights—and soured it with religious and racial bigotry. He directed some of his ire at Catholics; they would not be true Germans, he insisted, until they rejected Rome and embraced the Protestantism of Prussia. But Schönerer reserved his harshest words for Jews. His populist reforms, he declared in 1885, could be realized only with the "removal of Jewish influence from all sections of public life."

Such statements appealed to those who envied the dramatic advances

Jews were making in Austria. Emancipation came late to the Jews of the Habsburg Empire; they did not receive full civil rights until a new constitution was proclaimed in 1867. But once the barriers came down, Jews flocked to Vienna to take advantage of the educational and professional opportunities there. The Jewish population in the capital grew from 6,000 in 1860 to 147,000 in 1900, or to nearly nine percent of the whole. By the 1880s, Jews formed more than half the city's lawyers and physicians, and Jews owned the leading banks and department stores.

It was a dangerous time for success. Craftsmen in Vienna were losing out to volume manufacturers; shopkeepers could not compete with the department stores; an influx of cheap labor on the city's fringes kept wages low. It was all too easy for those threatened by these forces to blame the prosperous Jews. Adding to their anger was the fact that poor Jews—who far outnumbered the wealthy—were joining Jewish intellectuals in embracing Marxism. Thus Jews as a group were indicted on a bewildering array of counts: Reactionaries denounced them as revolutionaries; owners of failing businesses condemned them as capitalists; pan-German ideologues dismissed them as racial pollutants.

Christian zealots in Austria, meanwhile, revived ancient libels about Jewish ritual practices. One Catholic priest charged that Jews murdered Christians to use their blood in services. Another priest wrote a novel that foresaw daily hangings of hundreds of Jews until Vienna was free of them. His vision was not without foundation: A few rabid anti-Semites in Austria's noisy and largely ineffectual parliament stood up to ask for bounties on Jews, while other hatemongers advertised their sentiments with an insignia on their watch chains—a miniature Jew in a noose. None of this escaped Hitler, who carried the fetid assortment of anti-Semitic attitudes with him through his career. The persistence of those attitudes in his native land later helped him win supporters there.

In the Great War, sparked in 1914 by the assassination of the Habsburg heir, Archduke Franz Ferdinand, the Austrian and German empires joined forces in an epic struggle that ruined them both. In 1918, as the Habsburg dynasty collapsed in defeat, President Woodrow Wilson called for "autonomous development for the peoples of Austria-Hungary," a pledge that the empire's angry minorities and ambitious neighbors took advantage of. Parts of the former Habsburg domain formed the new states of Czechoslovakia and Yugoslavia. Other regions were reclaimed by Poland or meted out to Rumania and Italy. A reduced Hungary had to settle for independence. As for Austria proper, its plight was summarized by Georges Clemenceau, the French premier. "Austria," he said, "that's what's left over."

Little was left. An empire of 54 million subjects was reduced to a nation

At a 1929 artisans' parade, lissome comb and fan makers perform for an admiring crowd in front of Vienna's parliament.

A Last Waltz in Vienna

Vienna between the wars was a city determined to forget its troubles. After the defeat of Austria-Hungary in 1918, the glittering capital was left with only a fraction of its former empire and a burden of economic woes and political turmoil. The Viennese did their best to ignore these realities, however, and continued to pursue the good life that they had become accustomed to.

The cosmopolitan city, home of Mozart, Haydn, and Strauss, offered rich cultural gifts to its two million citizens. People flocked to the opera, symphony, and theater. They waltzed or fox-trotted nights away at dance halls and stately balls, crowded the smoke-filled cabarets, and debated at literary soirees.

Athletics captivated the Viennese, and the young people of the city competed vigorously in soccer, track and field, swimming, and other sports. At the same time, many citizens were content to while away the hours at their favorite coffeehouses or hike through Vienna's pine-scented woods. Others simply basked in the intoxicating beauty of the city's expansive parks and boulevards, its fabled Danube River, and its ornate architecture.

Events, however, were destined to eclipse the leisurely life in the capital. Hitler had decided to absorb the country of Austria into the Third Reich, and the successors to six centuries of Habsburg monarchs were too frail to resist.

Following an age-old tradition, a young girl arrives at the Prater amusement park in a flower-bedecked coach to celebrate her confirmation in the Catholic church. The 2,000-acre Prater was Vienna's recreational heart—a playground that included a landmark Ferris wheel, cafés, beer gardens, a racecourse, a polo field, and expanses of woods and marshland.

Baron Alfons Rothschild, the Austrian scion of the renowned European banking family, leads the 1932 Derby champion to the winner's circle at the Prater's Freudenau racetrack. More than 300 races were run annually at the Freudenau, a favorite gathering place for Vienna's elite; the Derby was a highlight of the social season.

Two Viennese matrons walk their prized borzois in a dog show on the capital's Ringstrasse in 1929. Every year, this grand circular boulevard was the site of dazzling pageants.

A military band performs at a *Kirtag*, or church festival, in Mauer, on Vienna's outskirts. Held in honor of a church's patron saint, a *Kirtag* featured music and dancing, along with sweets, toys, and souvenirs sold from decorated stalls.

of a mere 6.5 million inhabitants—2 million of them living in Vienna, where a cumbersome and costly bureaucracy remained in place. At the war's end, Austria had 233,000 civil servants with some 400,000 dependents—nearly a tenth of the country's population. They were a terrific drain on a state that had lost most of its natural wealth; the old empire's coal reserves now belonged to Czechoslovakia, and its richest farmland to Hungary.

Citizens of Austria could take solace in belonging to a culturally uniform state. Stripped of its ethnic provinces, the new nation was overwhelmingly German. This sense of identity brought with it a dilemma, however. Now, even more than before the war, Austrians felt that union with Germany was natural and necessary. Yet Germany, even in defeat, remained a nation of more than 60 million people and enormous potential. For Austria to come to terms with the giant to its north without being swallowed up would require an unprecedented level of trust between Berlin and Vienna. Briefly after the war, it appeared that such amity existed. The republics that emerged in Austria and Germany were dominated by Social Democrats—socialists who renounced the communists' revolutionary tactics. Austria's first postwar chancellor, socialist Karl Renner, called for Anschluss. But his efforts came to naught in 1919, when the victorious Allies imposed peace treaties on both countries that forbade their economic or political merger.

Compelled to fend for itself, the Austrian republic endured problems similar to those in Germany that contributed to Hitler's rise. Austria's Social Democrats, presiding over an economy in shambles, lost their majority in parliament in 1920. They never held power again nationally but remained a strong force in opposition. The leading figure in Austrian politics through most of the ensuing decade was Monsignor Ignaz Seipel, a Catholic theologian and head of Austria's conservative Christian Social party. As chancellor, Seipel restored Austria's treasury in 1922 through a huge loan guaranteed by the League of Nations. In return, however, he had to officially renounce the still-popular idea of Anschluss and impose austerity measures that cost tens of thousands of civil servants their jobs.

Such remedies did not make Seipel beloved in Austria, and growing tensions among Austria's federated states complicated his task. In the southeastern state of Styria, for example, which lost territory to Yugoslavia at the war's end, reactionaries dreamed of an autocratic pan-German empire. By contrast, the municipal state of Vienna remained a socialist stronghold; its leaders hiked taxes on the rich to fund controversial programs such as a working-class housing project known as the Karl Marx Hof. These efforts earned the city the label Red Vienna, a title that obscured the presence there of a sizable if straitened bourgeoisie, whose members upheld the capital's traditions as best they could. Narrow-minded Aus-

trians in the provinces regarded Red Vienna as a monolithic menace that betrayed the sinister influence of its alien elements, especially the Jews.

The ominous growth of rival paramilitary groups best expressed the factionalism in the republic. The Allies had restricted Austria to a standing army of 30,000 troops. This Volkswehr was a bone of contention from the start. Renner's socialists manipulated it in 1919 to put down a communist uprising. Later, Seipel's conservatives ousted the socialists from most command positions in the Volkswehr. Alienated and restive, the socialists developed their own irregular army, known as the Schutzbund. Mean-

Shirtless Austrian Storm Troopers lead their comrades through Vienna in 1933 to protest a ban on the wearing of Nazi uniforms. Such demonstrations imitated those staged earlier in Germany, reflecting the tendency of Austria's Nazis to take their cue from Berlin.

A poster disseminated by the Austrian right wing combines a caricature of a Jew and three arrows, symbol of the Social Democratic party. Anti-Semitism was so prevalent in Austria the socialists themselves exploited it in the 1920s, prompting thousands of Jews to quit the party.

while, militant bands of ultraconservatives were forming across the country to meet the leftist challenge. These home-defense forces, as they were called, sometimes feuded with one another before uniting in 1927 to yield a national Heimwehr. Many in this reactionary militia found inspiration in Mussolini—now Italy's dictator. But others were partial to the Austrian-born Hitler, whose campaign to seize power in Germany and forge a greater Reich was attracting increased attention in his native land.

Despite the presence of such sympathizers in the Heimwehr, the Austrian Nazi party in the late 1920s lacked the vigor of its German counterpart. This was ironic, because national socialism had been born in Austria-Hungary at the end of the Great War. A group calling itself the German National Socialist Workers' party had formed in April 1918 in the Sudetenland to protest the inclusion of that region in Czechoslovakia. The party's leader, lawyer Walter Riehl, urged that the Sudetenland declare itself an independent German state, to be ultimately included in a greater German Reich. Riehl's group, which shared the pervasive anti-Semitism of the pan-German movement, predated Hitler's Nazi party in Munich by nine months. For a while, the two parties progressed in tandem. Moving to Vienna to broaden his base, Riehl had registered 34,000 members by 1923. In elections that year in Hitler's boyhood home of Linz, the party took eight percent of the vote and four seats on the city council. But in an international Nazi conference at Salzburg in August, Riehl broke with Hitler when the Führer renounced political campaigning in favor of armed revolution. Riehl resigned as party chief, and the Austrian Nazis fell into disarray.

Riehl's successor, Karl Schulz, believed that his party could pursue goals similar to those of its German partner and remain independent. Such an idea was anathema to Hitler, who vented his fury in a parley with Schulz in 1925. Hitler "did all the talking," Schulz wrote later, "and the slightest objection was answered by him with a speech. After a two-hour interview, I still had not had a single opportunity to find out in concrete terms what Hitler expected of the Austrian movement." Schulz soon found out that Hitler expected utter fealty from his Austrian supporters. In 1926, the German leader announced the formation in Austria of the Hitler Movement, made up of unconditional loyalists. The power struggle among Nazis in Austria hurt the cause. In late 1928, Schulz's party numbered only

6,274 members, who defiantly wore gray shirts instead of brown; the Hitler Movement claimed just 4,446. With the depression's onset, however, the tide turned dramatically, and Hitler's Austrian loyalists surged to the fore.

In Austria as in Germany, the depression weakened an already-shaky democracy and strengthened totalitarian forces. Early in 1931, the government in Vienna tried to resuscitate the economy by accepting a German proposal that the two nations form a customs union, eliminating tariff barriers between them. France, however, denounced the plan as a violation of the 1919 treaties, and anxious investors began to withdraw deposits from the Kreditanstalt, the great Rothschild bank on which many smaller banks in Austria depended. Ultimately, the Kreditanstalt failed, and the plan for a customs union expired—a debacle for the Austrian government and a boon for its Nazi critics. In ostensibly Red Vienna, a Nazi organization with close ties to Germany exploited the crisis to appeal to the capital's unemployed masses. Party membership there mushroomed, from a mere 600 in 1930 to 40,000 three years later. Buoyed by such gains, the Nazis dreamed of an Austrian takeover to complement the one Hitler achieved in Germany in early 1933. But they would first have to reckon with an opponent who yielded little to Hitler in the way of cunning and who was passionately committed to Austrian independence.

As Hitler's triumph reverberated across Austria in February 1933, the nation's new chancellor, Engelbert Dollfuss, contemplated his own bold stroke. A diminutive man of peasant stock, the forty-year-old Dollfuss was proud and courageous, having served with distinction on the Italian front during the war. A member of the Christian Social party, he had watched with dismay in the 1920s as extremists undermined Chancellor Seipel's authority. Dollfuss was now prepared to take drastic steps, if necessary, to protect his government from its foes, whether Nazi or Marxist. He chose as justice minister a thirty-five-year-old lawyer who shared his ardent Catholicism and conservatism—the Jesuit-educated Kurt von Schuschnigg, whose dry, professorial manner belied his readiness to treat political heretics harshly. The tough tone of the new administration was signaled even more clearly by the man Dollfuss elevated to vice chancellor—Prince Ernst Rüdiger von Starhemberg, chief of the Heimwehr. The mercurial prince had once followed Hitler, taking part in his unsuccessful putsch in Munich in 1923, but had since chosen to operate within the Austrian political structure, albeit in a conspiratorial and high-handed fashion.

In March of 1933, a crisis in parliament presented Dollfuss with his cue for action. After a stormy session in which the assembly's three presiding officers had resigned one after another, Dollfuss refused to allow the legislature to reconvene. In succeeding months, he responded to Nazi violence by banning all Nazi activities and touting his new Fatherland Front as the nation's only legitimate party. Aware that Hitler was bent on annexing Austria, Dollfuss sought help from Mussolini, who promised to support Austria but demanded that the Fatherland Front take control of the state and crush the socialists. Dollfuss appeared eager to comply. Speaking in Vienna in September before a festive crowd decked out in Heimwehr uniforms and Austrian peasant garb, he proclaimed the death of parliament and denounced the socialists as the modern anti-Christ. His inflammatory language further antagonized the Left, which was already appalled at the blessing bestowed on Starhemberg and his Heimwehr.

Privately, Dollfuss still hoped to conciliate socialist leaders and thus bolster his government against the graver threat posed by the Nazis. But

Wall art in Vienna urges Austrians to "draw the line" against Nazi intimidation: "Protect your land, your home, and yourself." Such warnings became urgent in the early 1930s as Nazi agitators expanded their tactics to assassinations and bombings, using explosives smuggled from Germany.

the old feud between the Heimwehr and the socialist Schutzbund was escalating beyond his control. Matters came to a head early in 1934. On February 11, Major Emil Fey, Dollfuss's secretary for security and commander of the Vienna Heimwehr, informed his men, "Tomorrow we shall go to work, and we shall make a thorough job of it." The next day, Heimwehr units in Linz did just that, rounding up socialist leaders and seizing weapons caches. The action sparked an uprising by socialists in Vienna, and Dollfuss committed units of the regular army to put it down. On the second night of fighting, Justice Minister Schuschnigg denounced the rebels in a radio broadcast as "hyenas who must be driven from the country." A few socialist leaders did flee to Czechoslovakia, but most of their followers held fast, putting up a fierce if futile resistance. Residents of the Karl Marx Hof withstood a three-day siege by two infantry battalions backed by artillery before hoisting a white flag. The guns of February ended the socialists as an armed force and a municipal power in Vienna.

It was a Pyrrhic victory for Dollfuss. Far from solidifying his position, the conflict placed him at greater risk. Hitler's partisans in Austria smelled blood, and with their natural enemies on the left neutralized, they were ready to move in for the kill. The Austrian Nazis lacked a paramilitary force to rival the Heimwehr; their sizable but unruly contingent of Storm Troopers could hardly hope to succeed where the Schutzbund had failed. Instead, the Nazis would rely on a strike force armed and organized by the German SS—aided by sympathizers in the Austrian army, Heimwehr, and Vienna police—to carry out a coup. Hitler approved the plan in general terms. The assault was timed to catch Dollfuss and his cabinet in the Federal Chancellery at noon on July 25.

A few hours before that meeting, however, one of the Nazi conspirators on the Vienna police force, Johann Dobler, had a change of heart and blurted out details of the plot to acquaintances in a café. The news quickly reached Major Fey, who had recently been replaced as state security chief but remained in charge of the Vienna Heimwehr. Fey wasted precious time

A Nazi poster portrays Chancellor Dollfuss as a pied piper leading three scourges: Brutality *(top)*, Lies, and Murder. The Nazis feared Dollfuss for his readiness to stand up to their threats.

Dollfuss stands hat in hand at a state function with members of his cabinet, including Justice Minister Kurt von Schuschnigg *(far left)*. Critics, invoking the name of an earlier Austrian statesman of towering reputation, derided the five-foot-tall Dollfuss as Milli-Metternich.

confirming the report before warning the chancellor shortly before noon. Dollfuss dispersed his cabinet but remained in the chancellery. Minutes later, 150 troopers of SS Standarte 89, thinly disguised as police officers and soldiers, arrived in trucks outside the building. Dollfuss's new security chief, Baron Erwin Karwinsky, who was with him, saw through the ruse at once. "The 'soldiers' were obviously incorrectly dressed," he noted. "Some had rifles, some pistols; some had rifle straps, and some were without. Several had their weapons hanging simply by cords from their necks." Yet little could be done to meet this crude threat. Incredibly, the chancellery's guards were purely ceremonial—they carried no ammunition. The Nazis soon were in possession of the building.

At the last moment, Dollfuss tried to escape by a side door. It was locked. Turning back, he met a group of SS men led by Otto Planetta, who had served in the same regiment as Dollfuss in the war. Planetta fired two shots at close range, hitting Dollfuss in the armpit and neck. The shooting was apparently a calculated act, although the Nazis later claimed that Planetta had fired impulsively. The rebels laid the chancellor, mortally wounded but still conscious, on a sofa. Dollfuss asked for a priest, but his captors refused and berated him for spurning Hitler. Gazing up at his young inquisitors, Dollfuss answered them in the weary tones of a rejected patriarch, "Children, you simply don't understand." A few hours later, he died.

The taking of the chancellery was to signal the start of an uprising by Austrian Storm Troopers and Nazi partisans in the army and Heimwehr. But the Brownshirts held back, reluctant to risk their necks for their SS rivals, and the potential traitors in the Austrian armed forces refused to commit themselves, sensing that the coup had gone awry. Alerted by Dollfuss, most of his cabinet members had fled to the Defense Ministry, where they marshaled forces against the rebels. By late afternoon, the SS men in the chancellery had surrendered, and other conspirators—including a group that had seized control of a radio station—were being rounded up. In the weeks to come, the government imprisoned thousands of Austrian Nazis. For Hitler, it was a crushing setback. Any thoughts of trying to capitalize on Dollfuss's assassination were banished when he learned of Mussolini's reaction. The Italian leader had been hosting Dollfuss's wife and two children at his villa on the Adriatic when the coup was attempted. He rushed 50,000 additional troops to the Austrian border, which they threatened to cross if the Germans invaded.

On July 30, Austria's new chancellor, Schuschnigg, led the senior members of his government into Saint Stephen's Cathedral in Vienna for Dollfuss's requiem. Inside, soldiers knelt beside their machine guns, and double rows of troops carrying loaded carbines lined the aisles. It was a fitting start for a regime that hostile forces would besiege to the end. After the

Dollfuss's body rests on the sofa where Nazi assailants deposited him after storming the chancellery. Before he died, Dollfuss, who had once studied for the priesthood, offered his killers a benediction of sorts: "Children, be good to one another."

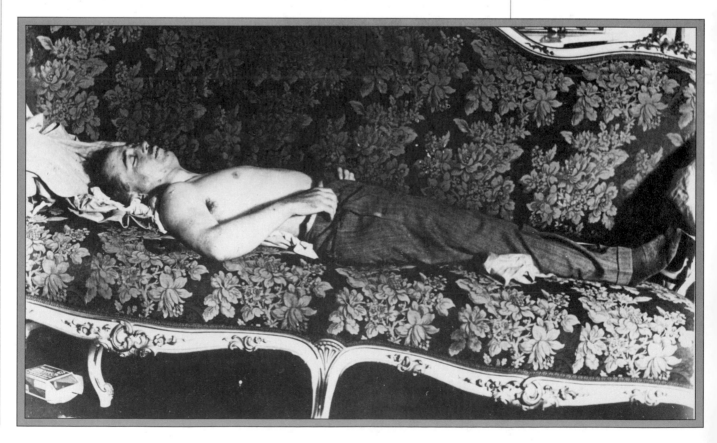

coup attempt, Schuschnigg proclaimed a new constitution, but he did not intend to restore democracy. The Fatherland Front remained Austria's only sanctioned party, one that would exert a benign but absolute authority in the sphere of politics, Schuschnigg reasoned, much as the Catholic church did in the realm of faith. This devout attitude alienated Schuschnigg from Hitler, who despised the Church. Yet the two leaders shared a fierce pride in their Germanic heritage. Schuschnigg, the son of a general in the Imperial Army of the Habsburgs, cherished the memory of the Holy Roman Empire—he called it a "great civilizing design." Such sentiments led him to hope for reconciliation with a Reich whose Führer he distrusted.

Suspecting that Austria's new chancellor might respond to diplomatic advances, Hitler shrewdly dispatched Franz von Papen, a former member of Germany's Catholic Center party, as his ambassador to Vienna. Papen made little headway at first, but events soon pushed Schuschnigg toward negotiations with Germany. In the spring of 1935, the Austrian government was encouraged to maintain its independence when Italy, France, and Great Britain formed the so-called Stresa Front to oppose any aggression by Germany. The front collapsed that autumn, however, when Italy invaded Ethiopia; after that, Mussolini looked increasingly to Hitler for support. The shift spelled trouble for the devious Prince Starhemberg, who as Schuschnigg's vice chancellor had been courting Mussolini. In the spring of 1936, Schuschnigg dismissed the prince. He sought to compensate for the loss of Starhemberg's Heimwehr by beefing up Austria's regular army and establishing an elite security guard—the blue-clad Sturmkorps.

Schuschnigg became convinced that he must come to terms with Germany. In July, he concluded an agreement with Papen. It seemed equitable on the surface: Germany recognized the full sovereignty of Austria and declared that the future of the Nazi party in Austria was a domestic affair in which Germany would not meddle. Austria acknowledged that it was a "German state" and implied that it would not join any anti-German alliance. However, these pledges were accompanied by unpublished articles, one of which constituted a major concession. Austria promised amnesty for all political prisoners, and within two weeks, some 17,000 Nazis were freed. The same covenant called on Schuschnigg to include in his government members of the "national opposition," a term that raised the specter of Nazis joining the chancellor's inner circle.

This problematic pact set the stage for the fateful conference between Schuschnigg and Hitler at the Berghof in February 1938. Some of the Nazis who were released from Austrian prisons in 1936 took part in fresh acts of subversion that included bombings and threats against Schuschnigg's life. Meanwhile, Berlin signaled that Hitler's pledge to respect Austrian sover-

eignty was an empty promise. Following the Hossbach conference of November 1937, at which Hitler had told his aides that he intended to annex Austria, Hermann Göring stepped up a personal campaign of intimidation aimed at inducing Austrian officials to yield without a fight. Foreign guests arriving that month for a sporting exhibition at Karinhall, Göring's hunting lodge outside Berlin, noticed that a huge fresco map of Europe on one wall there omitted the boundary between Germany and Austria. When the Austrian foreign minister, Guido Schmidt, drew attention to the fact, Göring explained, "Good hunters know no frontiers."

Göring was more direct with another Austrian guest, Peter Revertera, chief of security in the border state of Upper Austria. Göring assured him that Austria would be helpless before a German invasion. If Vienna would only accede to Anschluss, he went on, the capital could provide an "enormous reservoir of leader figures for the German people," and it would shine as the "cultural and artistic center of the Reich." Revertera took the next

Uniformed members of the Heimwehr, a paramilitary force loyal to Dollfuss, lead away Nazis who had seized a Vienna radio station during the coup attempt on July 25. The conspirators had broadcast a false report that Dollfuss had resigned in favor of Anton Rintelen, the Austrian ambassador to Italy and a Nazi sympathizer.

train back to Vienna to report the conversation to Schuschnigg. Göring had even revealed to him a target date for Anschluss: the spring of 1938.

Göring's deadline was no bluff. With or without Austria's cooperation, Hitler was intent on achieving the union soon, while international conditions were favorable. France's government was deeply divided and would be hard-pressed to mount an effective challenge to Anschluss. Britain, led by Prime Minister Neville Chamberlain, was contemplating new foreign-policy concessions to Germany in order to avert war. As always, the sight of a rival bearing the olive branch only encouraged Hitler in his aggressive designs. Mussolini's response to Anschluss was more problematic. Despite the recent rapprochement between the two dictators, Hitler had no guarantee that Mussolini would accept a German takeover of Italy's northern neighbor. To smooth the way, however, Hitler was prepared to acknowledge Italian sovereignty in the South Tyrol, a predominantly German-speaking area that Italy had wrested from Austria after the world war.

If Hitler's diplomatic strategy was clear, his tactics for the proposed takeover were as yet ill defined. Various options were open to him. Papen advocated an evolutionary approach, one that involved pressing Schuschnigg to share power with some of the less extreme Austrian Nazis until his adulterated regime gave in to annexation. Yet Papen was undercut by radical Nazis in Austria, who were fomenting a plot that fit Hitler's timetable. Their scheme, scheduled for April, included the murder of a leading German official by Nazis disguised as members of the Iron Legion, a group of Austrian monarchists intent on restoring to power the exiled Habsburg heir, Archduke Otto. Hitler, who loathed the Habsburgs as foes of German nationalism, had repeatedly stated that he would not tolerate such a restoration; the plot would thus give him a pretext for invasion. The prime candidate for assassination was Papen himself. Fortunately for the ambassador, the Vienna police uncovered the plot in mid-January of 1938. The discovery was a reprieve for both Papen and his diplomatic initiatives. Hitler, furious with the Austrian radicals for their bungling, had Papen invite Schuschnigg to a summit at the Berghof in February.

Reluctantly, Schuschnigg accepted, seeking to fend off the twin Nazi threats of subversion and invasion. He hoped that by offering Hitler further concessions, he could elicit a meaningful commitment to Austrian sovereignty. Before leaving Vienna, he drew up a list of the maximum concessions he was prepared to make. He was helped by Arthur Seyss-Inquart, a pan-German lawyer with Nazi sympathies who had joined the government as an opposition member. Schuschnigg trusted Seyss-Inquart in this advising role because he saw him as representative of those Austrians who wished to bring their nation closer to Germany without betraying it outright. Seyss-Inquart immediately violated that trust by communicating the concessions to Berlin. Thus Hitler knew in advance how much Schuschnigg was prepared to yield, knowledge that encouraged the Führer to press for more while offering little in return. The sorry episode summed up Austria's plight. After flirting so long with the idea of Anschluss, the country was being prodded to the altar by conspirators in its own camp. And the ceremony that loomed was looking less like a marriage than a sacrifice.

At half past nine in the morning on February 12, Chancellor Schuschnigg and Foreign Minister Schmidt left their sleeping car in Salzburg and traveled by limousine to the Berghof for the parley with Hitler. They were met at the border by a cheerful Papen, who informed them that three German generals had just arrived to meet with the Führer. Hitler could not have summoned a more intimidating trio—Walther von Reichenau, commander of the Fourth Army and advocate of German expansionism; Wilhelm Keitel, head of the Wehrmacht's high command; and Hugo Sperrle, Luftwaffe commander in Bavaria and former chief of the Condor Legion, whose raids in Spain had stunned the world. Papen assured Schuschnigg that the generals' appearance on the day of the conference was coincidence. Schuschnigg chose to accept this menacing departure from protocol and proceed. On the last leg of the journey, riding in a half-tracked reconnaissance vehicle up the icy slope to Hitler's retreat, he glimpsed new barracks for the Führer's SS guards—many of whom were recruits from Austria.

Hitler greeted his guests on the broad terrace of the Berghof, wearing a brown tunic and swastika armband. After introducing the Austrians to the three generals and his foreign minister, Joachim von Ribbentrop, the Führer took Schuschnigg aside and led him to his second-floor study, with its bracing vista. Schuschnigg politely complimented Hitler on the scenery, but the German was all business, assailing his guest in terms that Schuschnigg set down from memory after the conference. "Austria has never done anything that would be of any help to Germany," Hitler complained. "The whole history of Austria is just one uninterrupted act of high treason." Soon an indignant Führer was delivering bald threats: "I have only to give an order, and in one single night all your ridiculous defense mechanisms are blown to bits. You don't seriously believe that you can stop me or even delay me for half an hour, do you? Who knows? Perhaps you will wake up one morning in Vienna to find us there—just like a spring storm." Then, having brandished the stick, Hitler asked his guest to collaborate. "Besides my name, there are other great German names," he allowed. "We have a Hermann Göring. We have a Rudolf Hess. I offer you, Herr Schuschnigg, the unique opportunity to have your name added to these

Kurt von Schuschnigg, who succeeded Dollfuss as chancellor, addresses Austrian guild leaders in May 1935 as his vice chancellor, Prince Ernst Rüdiger von Starhemberg *(left)*, listens with arms crossed. Schuschnigg dismissed Starhemberg the following year, after he had praised Mussolini's invasion of Ethiopia "in the name of those who fight for fascism in Austria."

great German names. That would be an honorable deed, and all difficulties could be avoided." Schuschnigg declined, and the interview concluded.

The two heads of state then rejoined their aides for an awkward luncheon. "I sat opposite Hitler," Schuschnigg recalled. "We were served by exceptionally tall and remarkably handsome young SS men in snow white steward uniforms." Hitler spoke of his program to motorize the German army, and General Sperrle told of his experiences with the Condor Legion in Spain. Around two o'clock, Hitler excused himself. Schuschnigg was asked to await the Führer's summons. The chain-smoking Austrian chancellor took the opportunity to indulge his habit, one the abstemious Hitler could not abide. After two hours of suspense, Ribbentrop and Papen presented Schuschnigg and Schmidt with an alarming document—a list of demands that went far beyond the concessions Schuschnigg had been prepared to make. One item called for the Nazi sympathizer Seyss-Inquart to be appointed Austria's minister of the interior, with authority over the police and other security matters. Another insisted on the reinstatement of Nazis who had been dismissed from the army and the government. The goal of the demands was to grant Hitler's partisans license to impose their will in Austria. In return, Hitler promised merely to reaffirm in public what he had already acknowledged by treaty, Austria's right to independence.

A short time later, Schuschnigg was called to rejoin Hitler. He explained to the Führer that the demands could not be accepted on the spot since several required the approval of Austria's president, Wilhelm Miklas, who exercised prerogatives under the 1934 constitution. Indeed, Schuschnigg could not assure when the terms might be met. "At this answer, Hitler seemed to lose his self-control," Schuschnigg recalled. "He ran to the doors, opened them, and shouted, 'General Keitel!' Then, turning back to me, he said, 'I shall have you called later.'" The outburst was a ploy. Hitler had nothing to say to Keitel, but fetching him was ominous enough. When Hitler summoned Schuschnigg one last time, the Austrian chancellor was anxious to salvage what he could from this disastrous day and was relieved to find the Führer in a better mood. Hitler allowed Schuschnigg three days to secure approval of the new concessions, a few of whose terms had been softened to make the pill easier to swallow. "We can abide by this agreement for the next five years," he told Schuschnigg. "That is a long time, and in five years the world will look different, anyway."

As Schuschnigg returned with Schmidt to Vienna, he harbored few illusions about the value of Hitler's assurances. Reluctantly, he complied with the new demands, but his good faith went unrewarded. No sooner had Seyss-Inquart been appointed interior minister than he conferred in Berlin with Hitler, Göring, and Himmler. On his return, he issued a circular provocatively addressed "to the German police in Austria." Confident now that their transgressions would go unpunished, Austrian Nazis flaunted the swastika on flags and armbands and stepped up their subversive acts. On February 20, Schuschnigg was dealt another blow: Hitler, in a speech to the Reichstag, ignored his promise to reaffirm Austrian sovereignty. Instead, he referred menacingly to the suffering of the 10 million Germans living beyond the Reich's borders in Austria and the Sudetenland.

At last, Schuschnigg's patience was exhausted. On February 24, he appeared before parliament in his Sturmkorps uniform and pledged that Austria would never willingly surrender its national existence. To back up his words, he resolved to take his case for Austrian independence before the electorate. On March 9, he announced that on the following Sunday, March 13, a single question would be put before Austria's citizens: "Are you in favor of a free and German, an independent and social, a Christian and united Austria?" Designed to appeal to various groups within the electorate, the proposition was awkwardly phrased, but its thrust was clear. Schuschnigg was rallying the nation against Anschluss.

Word of the proposed plebiscite had an explosive impact in Berlin. On the morning of March 10, after conferring by phone with Göring, Hitler summoned Keitel and ordered him to prepare to invade Austria. That afternoon, he dispatched a letter to Mussolini, informing him of his determination to "restore law and order in my homeland."

At half past five the next morning, Schuschnigg in Vienna learned that the Germans had closed the border at Salzburg. Fearing the worst, he visited Saint Stephen's Cathedral on his way to the chancellery. "In front of the image of Our Lady of Perpetual Succor many candles were burning," he recalled. "I looked furtively around and then made the sign of the cross on the wire mesh protecting the sanctuary—an old Viennese custom in times of stress." At his office, he found a coded message from the Austrian consul general in Munich. It said simply, "Leo is ready to travel."

With this confirmation that invasion was imminent, Schuschnigg desperately tried to turn back the tide. Yielding to pressure from Berlin, he agreed that afternoon to call off the plebiscite, but this concession only drew a fresh demand from Göring: Schuschnigg must withdraw as chancellor in favor of Seyss-Inquart. Conceding defeat, the chancellor resigned, but President Miklas refused to call on Seyss-Inquart, and Schuschnigg remained in charge. His diplomatic options, never formidable, were exhausted. In recent weeks, he had clung to the hope that Mussolini might prevail on Hitler to stop short of invading Austria, but Mussolini, in his last communication to Schuschnigg, had warned against the plebiscite. France was in the midst of a change of administration and would be of little help. Britain informed Schuschnigg that it was "unable to guarantee protection."

Short of surrender, Schuschnigg had but one recourse: He could order Austrian troops to battle. In the end, he decided that such resistance would be not only futile but fratricidal. He explained later that as a proud German, he was determined to avoid the situation the Austrians had faced in 1866, when they fought the Prussians and were routed: "I refused to be instrumental—directly or indirectly—in the preparations for Cain once more to slay his brother Abel." Shortly before eight o'clock, after receiving a false report that Germans were crossing the border, he announced over the radio that he had instructed the Austrian army to yield: "We are resolved that on no account, and not even at this grave hour, shall German blood be spilled." Within minutes of Schuschnigg's broadcast, Hitler signed the invasion order. At quarter of eleven, he learned that he had Mussolini's blessing and responded gratefully that he would stand with the duce "through thick and thin." In Vienna, Miklas bowed to the inevitable and named Seyss-Inquart chancellor to preside over Austria's demise.

By dawn of the next day, March 12, troops of the German Eighth Army were pouring across the Austrian frontier unopposed. The border towns they entered had long been receptive to the Nazis, and in many of them crowds of civilians turned out to salute the occupiers. In Salzburg, well-wishers stood six deep in the snow to cheer the Germans. Hitler, meanwhile, flew to Munich with Keitel to oversee the operation. When he arrived there around noon, he had yet to decide on his next step. One option was to prop up Seyss-Inquart and his puppet regime, thus preserving a sem-

blance of Austrian autonomy. The ease of the invasion and the welcome the troops were receiving, however, suggested that such niceties might be dispensed with. Hitler decided to enter Austria himself to test the waters. That afternoon, riding in an open Mercedes-Benz, he crossed the border at Braunau, his birthplace, to a tumultuous welcome. A short time later, his motorcade reached Linz, where, at the age of sixteen, Hitler had quit school to spend his days roaming the streets, dreaming vaguely of glory. Now an estimated 100,000 of the city's 120,000 inhabitants turned out to hail his homecoming. Speaking from the balcony of the city hall, Hitler told of the vow he had made long ago to unite his native land with his adopted one: "I have believed in my task, I have lived for it, and I have fought for it, and you are all my witnesses that I have now accomplished it."

The cheers that greeted his words helped Hitler decide to assert absolute personal authority in Austria. As he spoke, Chancellor Seyss-Inquart stood by, having taken it upon himself to welcome Hitler to Linz "in the name of all Austrians." But Seyss-Inquart would soon be a forgotten man in the land he pretended to lead. Göring, who listened to the speech on the radio in Berlin, dispatched a brief message to Hitler that mirrored the Führer's sentiments and spelled the end for the last vestiges of self-rule in Austria: "If the enthusiasm is so great, why don't we go the whole hog?"

The next day, as German troops solidified their hold on Austria without firing a shot, Seyss-Inquart was presented with the draft of a law proclaiming Austria a province of the German Reich. He obligingly convened his cabinet and secured its approval. The balky Miklas then raised a final obstacle, refusing to sign the edict. Instead, he ceded his functions to Seyss-Inquart, who for a few moments thus occupied a dubious pinnacle as president and chancellor before signing the bill that abolished his government. One article of the law offered Austrians the

At left, the people of Salzburg turn out in force on March 12, 1938, to greet the invading Germans, including mountain troops with their packmules in tow. Below, a circle of exuberant schoolgirls welcome a sergeant from a German motorcycle unit.

opportunity to affirm Anschluss after the fact in a plebiscite on April 10.

Hitler next prepared for a triumphal entry into Vienna. He had hoped to travel there directly on March 13, after laying a wreath at his parents' grave in Leonding, outside Linz, but complications caused him to depart the next day. German motorized units were clogging the roads to Vienna; as the high command learned to its dismay, one-third of the army vehicles had broken down during the operation. And SS chief Himmler wanted an extra day to tighten security in Vienna—a task that was taking on major proportions.

Vengeful Austrian Nazis had begun rounding up their enemies on the eve of the invasion. Now, with the Germans in charge, the crackdown was being systematized. In Vienna alone, more than 70,000 people would soon be arrested by Himmler's agents, some to be held indefinitely in a new SS concentration camp located along the Danube at Mauthausen. A few of those targeted were prominent political figures. Former Chancellor Schuschnigg would spend ten weeks under house arrest in the capital, followed by seven years in various prisons. Many others were persecuted simply because of their heritage. For Vienna's large Jewish population, Anschluss meant the fulfillment of a threat that had been building for more than half a century. As crowds looked on and jeered, brown-shirted Nazis corralled Jewish men and women and forced them to scrub the capital's streets and clean its public latrines.

One Jewish family singled out for special attention was that of eighty-one-year-old Sigmund Freud, who had elected to remain in his homeland despite deep misgivings. (After he had learned of Schuschnigg's resignation on March 11, Freud wrote tersely in his diary, *Finis Austriae.*) When a contingent of Storm Troopers came to the Freud home, his daughter Anna surprised them by leading them to the family safe, opening it, and inviting them to make free with the contents like common thieves. At that moment, Freud himself looked in from an adjoining room and fixed his icy gaze on the intruders without saying a word. Flustered, the Storm Troopers left the family unmolested but promised that they would soon return. Duly warned, Freud and his family joined the 50,000 Jews who would flee the country in the months ahead after first surrendering some or all of their assets to the Nazis. A young, Austrian-bred SS functionary named Karl Adolf Eichmann, who would later commit many of the Jews who stayed behind to the death camps, supervised this mercenary emigration program.

In time, most Austrians would regret the day their land was joined to the Reich. But in the feverish onset of Anschluss, those who had nothing to fear from the Gestapo on political or racial grounds viewed the Führer as a messiah—a native son returning from exile to end years of strife and confusion. The reception that awaited Hitler in Vienna on March 14 re-

Adolf Hitler lays a wreath at his parents' grave in the Austrian town of Leonding on the morning of March 13. The homecoming was gratifying for Hitler, who had left Leonding thirty years earlier following the death of his mother. "I had honored my father," he wrote in *Mein Kampf,* "but my mother I had loved."

vealed a capital ready to embrace the new emperor, however dubious his lineage. As the British ambassador reported to London, "It is impossible to deny the enthusiasm with which both the new regime and last night's announcement of incorporation in the Reich have been received here."

Hitler's motorcade left Linz around eleven o'clock in the morning and made slow progress toward the capital along a route lined with admirers and littered with broken-down military vehicles. It took him more than six hours to cover the 120 miles to Vienna. The Führer entered the old imperial city in the dwindling light, standing ramrod straight in his car, stiffly returning the salutes of the crowd with his right arm. Nazi flags hung at every turn; even churches displayed the swastika. The cavalcade ended at the Imperial Hotel, which had once entertained Habsburg monarchs and their retinues. There Hitler took possession of the royal suite. Savoring the

Austrian Nazis force Jews in Vienna to scrub the pavement. Jews were put to work removing anti-Anschluss slogans from streets and walls with a mixture of water and acid that burned their hands.

Placards pasted to the rear of a convertible *(left)* urge Austrians to ratify Anschluss by voting yes in the April 10 plebiscite. A stern likeness of the Führer and explicit instructions on how to vote *(below)* greeted those who reported to the polls. More than 99 percent marked their ballots as they were directed.

moment, he told a few of his confidants how, as a young vagrant in Vienna, he had once cleared snow for meal money outside this same hotel. "We poor devils shoveled the snow away on all sides and took our hats off every time the aristocrats arrived," Hitler reportedly expounded. "They didn't even look at us, although I still smell the perfume that came to our noses. We were about as important to them, or for that matter to Vienna, as the snow that kept coming down all night, and this hotel did not even have the decency to send a cup of hot coffee to us."

Hitler's keen sense of retribution was heightened the next day when he stood on the balcony of the Hofburg, the former imperial palace, and addressed 200,000 Viennese in the square below. Before his dais rose two states of Habsburg royalty on their mounts. Spectators had scaled the monuments to see the Führer better. Taking for granted the result of the coming plebiscite, Hitler proclaimed the "conclusion of the greatest aim in my life, the entry of my homeland into the German Reich." Papen, who was with Hitler during the speech and the parade of German armed might that followed, described him as being in a "state of ecstasy."

At the risk of dampening the Führer's spirits, Papen warned Hitler that if he antagonized the Catholics in Austria as he had the Catholics in Germany, Anschluss might be imperiled. "Have no fear," Hitler replied, "I know that better than anyone." Hitler tailored his ensuing actions to prove the point. That evening, before leaving for Germany, he met with Vienna's Cardinal Theodor Innitzer, promising to respect the privileges of the Church in exchange for Innitzer's support in the April plebiscite. And when Hitler returned to Vienna on April 9 to whip up enthusiasm for the referendum the following day, his speech was cynically crafted to appeal to the devout. "I would now give thanks to him who let me return to my homeland in order that I might now lead it into my German Reich," the Führer intoned. "Tomorrow may every German recognize the hour and measure its import and bow in humility before the Almighty, who in a few weeks has wrought a miracle upon us!"

Such sermonizing was hardly necessary to secure a simple majority for the plebiscite. But Hitler wanted an overwhelming mandate, one he could wave before international critics as proof that Austrians welcomed their fate. And his campaign for a mandate did not depend on pious words alone. In Austria, as in Germany five years earlier, the first arrests made clear that dissent would carry a price. Morale among Hitler's opponents on the left eroded further when socialist Karl Renner, the former chancellor, grudgingly supported the plebiscite. Renner may have been motivated by concern for his colleagues being held by the Gestapo, and he had no kind words for the tactics Hitler used to achieve Anschluss, but he served Hitler's cause when he conceded, "The twenty years' stray wandering of the Austrian people is now ended." To make sure that Austrians stayed in line, the Nazis closely watched over the voting on April 10. A foreign journalist in Vienna noticed that slits in polling booths gave election officials clear views of citizens voting. Not surprisingly, the voters endorsed Anschluss by a vast margin. More than 95 percent of the electorate came to the polls. Of 4,453,000 ballots cast, scarcely 12,000 were negative.

When Hitler was told of the result, he called it the "proudest hour of my life." His professed passion for his homeland had been requited, albeit under duress. But he would not content himself for long with a single conquest. There was fresh quarry to be taken. ✠

On a mild April day, Germans and Austrians mingle at the Hochhaus, a popular rooftop restaurant in Vienna. The honeymoon was short. By fall, the Nazis had alienated much of the population by infringing on the rights of the Catholic church and Protestant minority and siphoning off commodities to Germany.

An Embrace of Dictators

When Adolf Hitler arrived in the country of Italy on a state visit early in May of 1938, he was delighted to find a welcome mat that stretched from the Brenner Pass to the Bay of Naples. Benito Mussolini had spared no expense in an effort to dazzle his fellow Axis dictator with Italian pomp and military might.

All along Hitler's railway route to Rome, buildings wore a fresh coat of whitewash. On May 3, the Führer arrived at a new train station built especially to receive him, and he entered the Eternal City on Viale Adolfo Hitler, a new road named in his honor.

The German chancellor was whisked from wreath layings to banquets, from Fascist rallies to brilliantly orchestrated military demonstrations. The breathtaking highlight of the five-day visit, a naval review in the Bay of Naples, featured 85 submarines that surfaced simultaneously to deafening salvos fired by the massed guns of 200 warships.

Hitler was impressed. Moreover, the visit succeeded in a way that Mussolini might not have anticipated: Hitler, like legions of tourists before him, fell in love with Italy. "The magic of Florence and Rome, of Ravenna, Siena, Perugia," he later recalled, "how lovely they are!" In Hitler's estimation, the smallest Florentine palazzo was "worth more than all of Windsor Castle," and the Italian people's instinctive artistry and their natural "Aryan" beauty, as he described it, were unparalleled. As for Mussolini, Hitler proclaimed him "one of the Caesars."

When the Führer left the Mediterranean land, the two leaders parted warmly; Hitler was reported to have had tears in his eyes. He returned to Germany confident that he had a staunch ally in the south. The duce was equally certain that the amity between the Axis nations would continue. "Henceforth," Mussolini exclaimed, "no force will be able to separate us."

Escorted by black-uniformed Italian police and Fascist militia, Mussolini and Hitler parade through the streets of Florence, which the Führer later described as his favorite Italian city.

...ens of Naples lean over their ...draped balconies to catch a ...se of the Führer. Hitler was ...not impressed with Neapoli-...n architecture; although he ...d never crossed the Atlantic, ...served that Naples might be ...nywhere in South America."

Wearing Renaissance costumes,
participants in a pageant of
traditional Tuscan sporting
events line up for the German
chancellor in the gardens of
the Pitti Palace in Florence.

A street approaching Florence's
fourteenth-century Palazzo
Vecchio bristles with Nazi
banners for Hitler's visit. The
Führer spent four hours viewing
paintings by old masters in
the nearby Uffizi Gallery, drag-
ging along a bored Mussolini.

After observing maneuvers by
the Italian air force and army,
Hitler and Mussolini picnic
under the gnarled seaside pines
of Santa Marinella, located
thirty-five miles from Rome.

Women dressed in provincial garb serve an alfresco luncheon for the two dictators—a sight that delighted Hitler, who waxed sentimental over the unspoiled beauty of the Italian people.

Mussolini, sniffing a rose, chats with Hitler on a Mediterranean bluff near Furbara, northwest of Rome, where Italian pilots displayed their skill by flying in swastika formation and dropping 150 tons of bombs on a mock town and two hulks at sea.

Military attachés in the uniforms of many nations—among them, Britain, France, Germany, and China—watch an artillery demonstration by Mussolini's army.

Seen from Hitler's vantage point on the flagship *Conte di Cavour*, Italy's warships maneuver in the dappled Bay of Naples against the silhouette of Vesuvius.

THREE

A Nation Sacrificed for Peace

Just two weeks after the German takeover of Austria, the militantly pro-Nazi Sudeten German party called half a million of its followers to rallies in the Sudetenland, the mountain-ringed uplands of western Czechoslovakia. In town after town, people filled the streets, the party's forbidden red and white flag flew over public buildings, and the crowds chanted, "One people, one Reich, one Führer!" In the town of Göckaulugun, the speaker proudly defied an order banning the Nazi salute. "On behalf of all," he cried, "I salute our Führer and the entire German people with upraised hand."

Among the ethnic Germans of the Sudetenland, the shock of the Anschluss loosed a surge of pan-Germanic feeling and demands for incorporation into the German state. Elsewhere in Czechoslovakia, however, news of Austria's capitulation to Hitler prompted dismay. Among citizens of Czech and Slovak descent, it roused not only fear for the future but stoic determination to preserve their state. The politicians in Prague saw the Anschluss as a prophetic warning of what would happen to small nations that tried to negotiate with Germany by themselves. For the army, it was the signal to prepare to fight. Wherever people stopped to talk—in cobblestoned village squares, in urban coffee shops, on Prague's winding streets, or on the graceful bridges across the Moldau River—they agreed their country was probably next on Hitler's list. Everywhere, citizens felt a chill of impending crisis and bewilderment about what had gone awry.

In some ways, Czechoslovakia inherited at birth the crisis that it faced in 1938. No Hitler loomed on the horizon then, but the potential for German-Czech conflict was clear. When Czechoslovakia was created after the world war from elements of the Austro-Hungarian Empire, the new state protruded deeply into German territory. This gave German propagandists the opportunity to portray the fledgling nation as a spearhead in Germany's side and a threat to the German heartland. Moreover, the Reich coveted Czechoslovakia for its strategic location, which dominated central Europe.

Czechoslovakia's fractious minorities made the country even more vulnerable. Of its 15 million people, about half were the Czechs of Bohemia

Following Germany's seizure of Czechoslovakia in March 1939, a Czech police officer in the city of Brünn obeys an order to change a street sign from "Freedom Avenue" to "Adolf Hitler Place." The occupiers Germanized even Czech traffic patterns, requiring motorists to switch from the left to the right side of the road.

and Moravia, and one-fourth were Slovaks living mainly in Slovakia. The rest were Germans, Hungarians, Ukrainians, and Poles. Although the government pursued an evenhanded minority policy, many of these peoples felt isolated from their ethnic roots and resented the politically and economically dominant Czech-Slovak majority. Many of them felt the pull of other nations. Hungary had strong ethnic and economic ties to the eastern part of Slovakia and the province of Ruthenia. Poland had claims on the former duchy of Teschen, a coal-rich, heavily Polish area on Czechoslovakia's northern border. Most troublesome of all, however, was the connection between Hitler's Reich and the more than three million Germans living in the Sudetenland. When Czechoslovakia was formed, its leaders insisted that the mountain area be included in their country for defensive reasons. The people came with the territory.

The Sudeten Germans were descendants of Germanic migrants who had come into Bohemia and Moravia in the twelfth century. After the establishment of Habsburg rule over Bohemia and Moravia in the sixteenth century, the tide of Germanic migration swelled—and so did German dominance over the Czech population. When the German flood finally subsided in the nineteenth century, the Sudeten Germans feared being eventually engulfed by the Czechs and fiercely opposed all Czech efforts at autonomy. With this history of mutual suspicion, the Sudeten Germans and the Czechs suddenly found their roles reversed. When the Paris Peace Conference established the boundaries of Czechoslovakia in 1919, the Sudeten Germans were no longer a dominant group looking toward Vienna but simply a linguistic minority governed by Czechs and Slovaks in Prague. Inevitably, the Sudetens resented their submission, particularly to people of Slavic descent, to whom most Germans felt racially superior.

When the depression arrived late in the 1920s, many people in the predominantly industrial Sudetenland lost their jobs—particularly after cheap textile exports from Japan flooded the world market and forced Sudeten mills to close down. Sudetens blamed their misfortune on the government, and their frustration spawned a spectrum of ethnic German political parties. The more moderate of these parties called for better markets for Sudeten

Czechoslovakia's founding fathers, Tomáš Masaryk *(right)* and Edvard Beneš *(left)*, share a warm moment with the visiting French foreign minister, Jean-Louis Barthou, in 1934. During the struggle to preserve Czechoslovak independence, Beneš became known as "Europe's smartest little statesman."

A Patchwork of Peoples

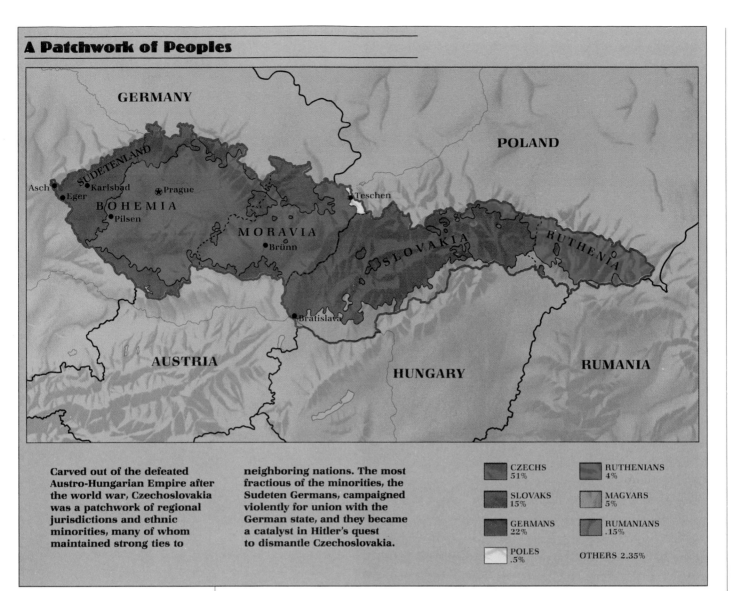

Carved out of the defeated Austro-Hungarian Empire after the world war, Czechoslovakia was a patchwork of regional jurisdictions and ethnic minorities, many of whom maintained strong ties to neighboring nations. The most fractious of the minorities, the Sudeten Germans, campaigned violently for union with the German state, and they became a catalyst in Hitler's quest to dismantle Czechoslovakia.

CZECHS 51%
SLOVAKS 15%
GERMANS 22%
POLES .5%
RUTHENIANS 4%
MAGYARS 5%
RUMANIANS .15%
OTHERS 2.35%

products and modest concessions to Sudeten autonomy—all-German police and German regional officials, for example. More extreme right-wing groups, such as the Sudeten German National Socialists, aped the Nazi party and wanted to break away from Czechoslovakia entirely.

In 1935, the Nazi regime in Germany began to subsidize the ultraright Sudeten German party. The party's leader was Konrad Henlein, a thirty-six-year-old war veteran and former bank clerk. With German support, Henlein gradually eclipsed more moderate German nationalist leaders and made himself the leading spokesman for Sudeten German grievances.

During this tense time, a strong advocate of nationalism took charge of the government in Prague. In December 1935, Edvard Beneš was elected Czechoslovakia's president, succeeding his compatriot, Tomáš Masaryk. A small, wiry man, the son of peasants, Beneš had shown political brilliance when he and Masaryk together sought and won Czechoslovakia's independence at the end of the world war. A realist with no illusions about Hitler's ambitions, Beneš knew that Czechoslovakia could survive in the cauldron of central European politics only if its defenses were strong and its alliances reliable. And at the moment, his country depended on an untested and extremely fragile structure of agreements. Much hinged on the attitude of France. If the French stood firm in honoring the mutual military-assistance treaty they had signed with Czechoslovakia in 1926, the Czechs could possibly count on English support as well. Although the British had no treaty with Czechoslovakia, they were bound by the Locarno Pact of 1925 to come to the aid of the French if they were attacked by Germany. Czechoslovakia had also made a pact with the Soviet Union in May 1935, only days after France had signed a similar treaty with the Russians. An important provision of the Czech-Soviet treaty held that neither country was obliged to go to the other's aid unless France had already done so. If France abandoned Czechoslovakia, Russia could, too. Finally, Czechoslovakia had treaties with Rumania and Yugoslavia, its partners in the Little Entente. This alliance, supported by France, united the three signatories against Hungarian territorial claims on all three nations.

Beneš realized that this edifice of alliances could collapse at any moment. Hitler suspected the same thing, and he set out to undermine the structure. Until he secured Austria and built up his own strength—until he had a "platform from which to shoot," as one German diplomat baldly put it— Hitler would not invade Czechoslovakia. Instead, he launched a propaganda attack to discredit the government in Prague, diplomatically isolate Czechoslovakia, and provide an excuse for aggression.

Anti-Czech propaganda played shrewdly on Western fears of Soviet power by labeling Czechoslovakia an "outpost of bolshevism" that was covered with airfields for the launching of bombing attacks on Germany. Moreover, the Nazis claimed that Sudeten Germans were being mistreated—starved and tortured, according to Reich press reports—and maintained that Germany owed them protection. Meanwhile, German officials rattled their sabers. Czechoslovakia was nothing but the "vermiform appendix of Europe," Hermann Göring sneered to the French ambassador. "We shall have to operate!"

On the heels of the Anschluss, Hitler increased the pressure on the Czechs. In Berlin on March 28, 1938, the Führer told Henlein that the Sudeten German party must make demands that the Prague government could never satisfy. At all costs, the party should avoid being trapped in a political settlement that would deprive Germany of its excuse to attack.

Before he left Berlin, Henlein received a new list of imperatives to present to Prague. In a fiery speech to the Sudeten Party Congress in Karlsbad on April 24, surrounded by hundreds of militant followers in gray uniforms and boots, he demanded complete administrative autonomy for the Sudetenland and compensation for wrongs inflicted on the German minority since 1918. In addition, he insisted that Prague accept the Sudetenland's right to embrace the Nazi ideology and maintain ties to the Third Reich. In the view of the Czech government, most of the Karlsbad demands were impossible to negotiate, much less to grant.

Around the time of Henlein's Karlsbad speech, Hitler took another step toward his goal of conquest. On April 21, he gave General Wilhelm Keitel, chief of the Wehrmacht high command, preliminary orders for Plan Green, the invasion of Czechoslovakia. Meanwhile, the Western powers grew increasingly alarmed over the Sudeten situation and all that it portended. On April 28, Prime Minister Neville Chamberlain of Britain and Premier Édouard Daladier of France met at 10 Downing Street in London to discuss how to preserve the peace.

What emerged from the lengthy meeting was less a plan of action than

At left, militant workers shoulder their tools beneath banners heralding May Day in a 1935 poster that promises "work, rights, and bread" to voters who support the Sudeten German party. Such socialistic appeals reflected the pro-Nazi party's outreach to the many Sudeten Germans idled by the depression or eking out a living in the region's slums, shown below.

an expression of helplessness. The British and French agreed only that they would let Berlin know they were vigorously pressing Prague to make generous new concessions to solve the Sudeten crisis. But coming to Czechoslovakia's aid with force seemed out of the question. The British chiefs of staff had reported to Chamberlain that supplies of their armaments were so short and the condition of the British army and air force so poor that war in 1938 would mean almost-certain defeat. The British had scarcely any antiaircraft guns or radar units for defense against enemy bombers. The British army could field only one armored brigade and five divisions of troops. Moreover, in the event of war, Britain could not count on aid from the United States, which had adopted a policy of strict neutrality to avoid involvement in another European conflict.

France, it was true, had seventy divisions, and Czechoslovakia itself had a standing army of about fifteen divisions—205,000 crack troops. In addition, the Czechs had fortifications along their frontier with Germany comparable to the Maginot Line and could rely as well on their giant Skoda armaments works. Against these resources, Germany could muster about seventy divisions backed by the most powerful and modern armaments industry in the world. What worried the French was not so much the present size of German forces as the manpower pool behind them. With a population of more than 70 million, compared with 40 million in France, the Germans could increase their forces by seven divisions a month.

And the Luftwaffe gave the Germans a decided psychological edge because Western statesmen feared the bombing of civilians. In fact, the

German air force was not designed for long-range strategic bombing, but its advantage in numbers and performance was impressive. Germany could put more than 2,800 modern planes in the air. In contrast, 1,200 mostly antiquated aircraft were available to the Royal Air Force, and the French and Czechs each had only 700. British and French aircraft industries also lacked the manufacturing capability to make up large losses, while German factories were capable of turning out more than 700 planes a month.

Early in May, Hitler paid a state visit to Italy *(pages 74-81)* and won Mussolini's assurance that the Italians had no objection to a German move against Czechoslovakia. Later that month, British and French leaders had more reason than ever to regret their military shortcomings. On May 19, London and Paris received reports of German troops advancing toward the Czechoslovak frontier. On that same day, Henlein broke off talks with the Prague government and departed for Austria, ostensibly to take his wife on vacation. Rumor had it, however, that he left to confer with Hitler and would return with the invading Germans. In the Sudetenland, word spread that there was no point in buying Czech postage stamps because they would be useless after the invasion. The Prague cabinet took the reports seriously enough to call up about 174,000 reservists and move troops into the border areas. The presence of the troops stanched the sporadic brawling between Sudeten Nazis and Czech police that had plagued the Sudetenland for weeks. Still, there were casualties. On May 21, two Nazis on motorcycles ignored a command to halt at a checkpoint in the town of Eger. A guard opened fire, and the men were killed. The incident provoked no further violence but provided the Sudeten Nazis with two martyrs. In Berlin, Foreign Minister Joachim von Ribbentrop blustered and threatened. "In Czechoslovakia, they are now starting to shoot down Germans!" he raged at the British ambassador, Sir Nevile Henderson.

During the crisis, the British and French made no commitments. Lord Halifax, the British foreign secretary, warned Ribbentrop that Britain might intervene if war erupted but told the French not to count on it. The French foreign minister, Georges-Étienne Bonnet, said that a German invasion of Czechoslovakia would "automatically" start a war, but he confided to the British that if the Czechs refused to make concessions to Hitler, France would consider itself free of its treaty obligations. Bonnet was haunted by a vision of German air attacks destroying Paris "meter by meter."

By May 23, it had become clear that the German army was not going to attack. In the aftermath of the scare, Bonnet deplored the "useless provocation" of the Czech mobilization and thanked the German government for its "dignified and calm restraint." Chamberlain believed that the Germans had actually intended to invade and that British warnings had

stopped them. Hitler, meantime, angrily noted the efficiency of Czech mobilization and grew more convinced than ever that Czechoslovakia must be destroyed soon—by a lightning strike.

Hitler told his military chiefs that they would invade Czechoslovakia on October 1. Soon thereafter, the Wehrmacht would do an about-face, attack the Western powers, and drive to the English Channel. Hitler felt that the time was right for starting a war. He had concluded that the Wehrmacht would never be stronger against the forces of his potential enemies. Waiting would only allow them to rebuild their armies and bolster their defenses.

Hitler had dismissed the possibility that his other prospective foe, the Soviet Union, would enter the war as Czechoslovakia's ally. Josef Stalin had purged the Soviet officer corps in 1937, badly weakening the army's command system. It was also unlikely that Russian forces would be allowed to cross the territories of Rumania and Poland to reach the Czechoslovak frontier. In fact, Hitler was not alone in his analysis of the Soviets; diplomats of all the major European powers had concluded that Stalin was determined to stay out of war.

The Führer's ambitions drew immediate objections from the chief of the army general staff, General Ludwig Beck. The Wehrmacht was not ready for

Arms production at the sprawling Skoda plant in the Czech province of Bohemia surpassed that of any European factory except the Krupp Works of Germany. The Skoda plant specialized in heavy guns but also turned out aircraft, tanks, railroad engines, tractors, marine propellers, and ammunition such as the gleaming brass 150-mm cannon shells being inspected by a worker at right.

war, Beck warned, and would not be until 1941. But General Walther von Brauchitsch, commander in chief of the army, did not support Beck, and Hitler refused to alter his plans. Many German officers of high rank shared Beck's reservations about the prospect of war. In fact, discontent and talk of resigning was so rampant that Brauchitsch assembled the army chiefs and warned them not to desert their posts while the attack on Czechoslovakia was imminent. Nevertheless, Beck resigned his command.

While Hitler moved implacably toward war, the British and French alternately cajoled and bullied the Czechs to extract the concessions they believed would keep the peace in Europe. Henlein's Karlsbad demands, the British now maintained, should be accepted virtually in full. Reporting to Washington, William Bullitt, American ambassador to France, protested that the Czechs would prefer a "conflagration that will destroy all Europe, rather than make the large concessions that alone would satisfy Hitler."

To prod the Czechs, Chamberlain sent a personal envoy to Czechoslovakia. He chose Walter Runciman, a sixty-eight-year-old millionaire shipbuilder and member of Parliament. A small, taciturn man, Runciman seemed to belong to the nineteenth century. He wore stiff, winged collars and a top hat even in the sweltering August heat.

The envoy said he was in Prague as a "friend of all and an enemy of none," but the correspondents there knew better. The journalist William L. Shirer jotted in his diary that Runciman intended "to gum up the works and sell the Czechs short if he can." In fact, Chamberlain had not even bothered to consult Beneš before sending the mediator. The Czech president and his prime minister, Milan Hodža, were appalled, but publicly they accepted the mission as a gesture of goodwill.

From the day Runciman arrived, he was besieged by delegations from the Sudeten German party anxious to present their grievances. Very quickly he decided that Beneš did not "show much sign of an understanding or respect for the Germans in Czechoslovakia." Runciman toured the Sudetenland, where carefully rehearsed crowds cried, "Give us a just solution, Lord Runciman!" He met with Henlein and came away convinced that he was a man of peace who wanted only autonomy for his people. Frank Ashton-Gwatkin of the British Foreign Office, a member of the Runciman party, told London how much he liked Henlein: "He is, I am sure, an absolutely honest fellow."

Runciman concluded that Czechoslovakia's only course was to accommodate Henlein by responding to the Karlsbad demands. On September 5, the government nearly did just that. Worn down by pressure from the British and French, the Czech cabinet produced the Fourth Plan, proposals that adhered to the Karlsbad demands so closely that negotiators for the Sudeten German party were astounded and dismayed. Suddenly, it seemed the ground was being cut from under Henlein and the Nazis, and the carefully crafted excuse for German intervention was disappearing.

Henlein's lieutenants, however, were equal to the situation. On September 7, they provoked a confrontation in the town of Mährisch-Ostrau between hostile Sudetens and Czechs. Sudeten propaganda distorted police efforts to maintain order into a brutal picture of innocent citizens being thrashed with whips and pinned against walls by police horses. The Sudeten German party suspended negotiations with the government.

Beneš went on the air to appeal for "goodwill and mutual trust" between Sudeten and Czech. "I do not speak through fear of the future," he said. "I have never been afraid in my life." The Sudeten German party responded to his plea by igniting riots. Eighteen people were injured in Eger, and police were besieged in their station house in Reichenberg.

All those concerned waited anxiously for the speech Hitler was to give to the Nazi rally at Nuremberg on September 12. On that evening, the streets of Prague were deserted. Czechs sat at their radios, listening to the familiar, rasping voice with its hint of hysteria. Correspondent Shirer wrote that the Führer's voice was full of hate, rousing his audience to the "borders of bedlam." He prefaced a long recital of alleged wrongs against the Sudetens with the chilling warning, " 'Ich spreche von der Tschechoslowakei!'—I speak of Czechoslovakia—his words, his tone, dripping with venom."

On the day after Hitler's speech, rioting broke out in scores of Sudeten towns. Jewish and Czech shops were sacked, swastika banners were unfurled, and Czech street signs were painted out and the swastika painted over them. In the town of Eger, police stormed Henlein's headquarters in the Hotel Victoria, killing six of the defenders. Prague restored order only after declaring martial law and sending troops into the Sudetenland. On September 14, Chamberlain dispatched a telegram to Hitler, asking for a face-to-face meeting. In Prague, newsboys shouted derisively, "Extra! Extra! The mighty head of the British empire goes begging to Hitler!" Hitler confided later that he was "astounded," but he replied promptly that he

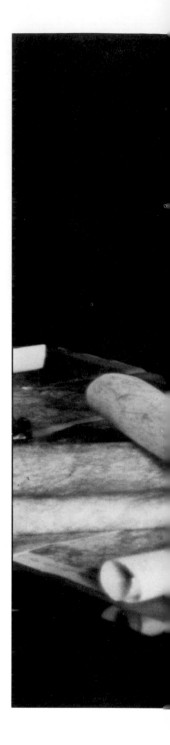

Generals Jan Syrový (left) and Emil Krejči study maps of the Czech frontier with Defense Minister František Machnik.

Defiant Defenders of the Frontier

A military invasion of Czechoslovakia would have run head-on into a defense more ferocious than Adolf Hitler or his generals anticipated. Soldier for soldier, the Czech army, led by a pair of hard-bitten world-war veterans *(above)*, was as efficient as the Wehrmacht and was superbly equipped with hundreds of 150-mm howitzers and other artillery from the famed Skoda arms works. The infantry had a machine gun for every twenty troops, the highest firepower ratio of any army in the world in 1938.

More daunting was the network of hidden forts and concrete gun emplacements that the Czechs, at a cost of $500 million, had tunneled into the Erz and Sudetic mountains guarding the border with Germany. So strong and cleverly sited were these defenses that German officers, examining them later, were appalled at the thought of what an attack would have cost. Even Hitler was shaken. "We had run a serious danger," the Führer admitted. "The plan prepared by the Czech generals was formidable."

Their mountain howitzers carried by mules, Czech artillerymen climb into hills that offer deadly fields of fire at attackers crossing the plain below.

Czech defenders file into a concrete-reinforced trench, part of the "little Maginot Line" that was established just inside the border with Germany.

Dug into a mountaintop foxhole, a Czech soldier aims one of the army's excellent 7.92-mm light machine guns. The armaments works at Brünn could turn out 25,000 of these weapons a year.

would receive the British prime minister at Berchtesgaden the following day. War was imminent, Chamberlain felt, and he must make a last-minute effort to avert the tragedy. The Czech riots demonstrated that Runciman had failed. Henlein, fleeing to Germany, had issued a proclamation calling for German annexation of the Sudetenland, and Prague had ordered his arrest as a traitor. British Commonwealth countries, unprepared to fight for Czechoslovakia, were pressuring London to avoid war.

At the same time, the French government was showing signs of panic; an alarmed Daladier called London to beg Chamberlain to make whatever appeal he could to save the peace. National leaders in Paris and London had received frightening reports from their envoys describing Germany's preparations for war. They learned that tens of thousands of workers had been assigned to bolster Germany's West Wall defenses. Men of military age were being refused permission to leave Germany; saleswomen were reporting to the Labor Service for emergency duty; food supplies near the western frontier were being moved to the interior; railroads were refusing commercial freight because of the burden of military traffic. Hitler was indeed preparing for war. Field units would move forward on September 28. On the invasion day—now tentatively set for September 30—200,000 troops poised for attack would swing toward the Czech frontier.

As Chamberlain made his way to Berchtesgaden on September 15, he did not know that Hitler had chosen a date for invasion, but he feared the worst. On his first airplane trip of any length, the prime minister flew to Munich, then motored up to Hitler's aerie in the Bavarian Alps, in the southeast corner of Germany not far from Austria. The journey took seven hours, and it was four o'clock in the afternoon when the sixty-nine-year-old Chamberlain arrived, weary from travel. Hitler was waiting to meet him on the Berghof steps, and the two men went into Hitler's study to drink tea and talk, with only Hitler's interpreter present. On this first meeting, the two heads of government did not impress each other. Chamberlain thought Hitler looked like the "house painter he once was," and Hitler considered Chamberlain an "insignificant" man whose only real interest was fishing.

Hitler rambled on about the injustices of the Versailles treaty and what he had done to redress them. All the while, he had pursued a policy of peace in Europe, the Führer asserted, but the case of the Sudeten Germans was special because it touched on the basic racial convictions of the German people. And he was absolutely prepared to start a world war, if necessary, to bring the Sudetenland into the Reich. Chamberlain asked about the Sudeten areas of mixed nationality and other concerns, but the questioning only irritated Hitler. "I want to get down to realities," he

Bystanders survey the twisted wreckage of two automobiles destroyed in a 1938 grenade ambush that killed the cars' occupants near the Sudeten border town of Graslitz.

shouted. "Three hundred Sudetens have been killed!" The weary Chamberlain began to get angry. "If the Führer is determined to settle this matter by force," he snapped, "why did he let me come here?"

That calmed Hitler somewhat. A peaceful solution might still be possible, he mused, provided that Britain agreed to the cession of the Sudetenland. Chamberlain said he personally "recognized the principle of the detachment of the Sudeten areas" but would have to consult his cabinet and the French government. Extracting a promise from Hitler not to act until they met again, he left for Munich and the flight home. The prime minister had not mentioned consulting the Czechs. At the airport in England, cheering crowds greeted Chamberlain. He told them that his talk with Hitler had been frank and friendly: "I feel satisfied that each of us fully understands what is in the mind of the other." The crowd shouted, "Good old Neville!"

On September 18, Daladier and Bonnet came to London to learn what had happened at Berchtesgaden and what the British proposed. The only solution to the problem of Czechoslovakia, Chamberlain told them, was for Prague to cede to the Reich any areas in which Germans composed at least half the population. The French, after arguing for a few hours, agreed. After all, said Bonnet to the American ambassador, Bullitt, they could not let Beneš "drive 40 million French people to their deaths in order to maintain the domination of 7 million Czechs over 3.5 million Germans." When Bonnet gave the news of this mutual proposal to Stefan Osusky, the Czech minister to France, Osusky wept. "My country has been condemned without a hearing," he complained to waiting journalists.

The Prague government had been dubious about the Berchtesgaden mission from the beginning. It reflected, said the Czech ambassador to London, the "senile ambition of Chamberlain to play the peacemaker." And the outcome was even worse than they had imagined. They argued desperately that cession of the Sudetenland would mean the loss not only of much of their industrial capacity but of their frontier fortifications as well. In effect, it would leave them defenseless. The Anglo-French reply, however, was an ultimatum, delivered to Beneš at two o'clock in the morning on September 21: If the Czech government refused their proposal, Britain and France would no longer consider themselves responsible for the fate of Czechoslovakia. Realizing that he was being abandoned, the weary Beneš convened his cabinet at half past six, and by late afternoon the Czechs had agreed to cede the Sudetenland to Germany. "We had no choice," Beneš said bitterly. "We have been basely betrayed."

Hitler, meanwhile, continued his preparations for war. The day after his meeting with Chamberlain, he authorized the establishment of the Sudeten German Free Corps, made up of hoodlums whose mission was to create havoc in the Sudetenland by staging terrorist raids across the border. On September 18, the German high command gave Hitler its final plan for the deployment of five armies against the Czechs. With Hitler's blessing, the Poles presented a note to the Czech government on September 21 demanding that the Teschen district, with

Prime Minister Chamberlain of Britain (*foreground*) and Foreign Minister Ribbentrop of Germany peer into the dappled waters of the Chiemsee, a lake southeast of Munich, during a break on Chamberlain's return trip to England after his first meeting with Hitler in September 1938.

its large Polish population, be ceded to Poland. A day later, Hungary demanded that Prague cede the provinces of Ruthenia and Slovakia, plus all Magyar-inhabited areas. By that day, the Sudeten German Free Corps had seized the Czech towns of Eger and Asch.

Also on that day, the optimistic Chamberlain met with Hitler again, this time at the town of Bad Godesberg on the banks of the Rhine. There the prime minister was surprised to hear cheers of "Heil Chamberlain!" from people in the street. Newspapers had been telling the populace that the Führer and the prime minister were working night and day for peace.

This time, the meeting went badly almost from the start. Chamberlain had hardly finished outlining the Anglo-French proposal for the transfer of the Sudetenland when Hitler remarked, in a strangely quiet voice, that this was no longer enough. Chamberlain listened in astonishment while the Führer said Czech oppression had grown so severe that strategic areas of the Sudetenland must be occupied at once. All Czech army troops, police officers, and administrative officials must immediately withdraw from the zones to be occupied. The Germans would pay nothing for the state property they took over, and Hitler would refuse to sign a nonaggression pact with Prague until the Hungarian and Polish claims against Czechoslovakia were also satisfied. When Chamberlain pressed for details about the dimensions of the occupied zone, Hitler shouted that the only important thing now was speed, to prevent Czechoslovakia from becoming a Bolshevik state. Later, as he stood with Chamberlain on the terrace of the Hotel Dreesen, Hitler's truculent mood changed; he apologized for the evening mist that obscured a beautiful view of the Rhine he had particularly wanted the prime minister to see.

The next day, Hitler gave Chamberlain a memorandum listing his demands, and he named October 1 as the deadline for Czech evacuation of zones to be occupied in the Sudetenland. Chamberlain promised to pass the new demands to the Czech government but committed himself to nothing more. News that the conference was not going well had leaked in Bad Godesberg, and a pall fell over the international contingent assembled in the town. An observer noted that even Joseph Goebbels and Hermann Göring seemed "plunged in gloom."

In the aftermath of the conference, Europe braced for war. The Czechs rejected the new German demands. On British and French advice, the Czech government had refrained from complete mobilization during the early stages of the Godesberg negotiations, but on September 23, Prague called to arms all reserves under the age of forty—an additional million troops. Across the border, thirty German divisions moved into position to attack. French reserve units were dispatched to positions along the Maginot Line. The British mobilized their fleet and warned their dominions to expect war. Slit trenches were dug in Hyde Park, and Chamberlain's closest adviser, Sir Horace Wilson, was dispatched to tell Hitler that Britain and France would fight for Czechoslovakia.

In two stormy sessions with Wilson, Hitler threatened to invade by September 28 if the Czechs did not agree to his peaceful occupation of the Sudetenland. He told Wilson to come to the Berlin Sportpalast that night to hear him address the nation; there the British envoy would gain a sense of the resolute mood of the German people. What Wilson witnessed instead was Hitler's manic recklessness, a sobering picture of a man on the verge of losing control. Shouting and shrieking, Hitler delivered a diatribe against Czechoslovakia—a state, he said, that had begun with a lie whose father "was named Beneš." He had seen Czech persecution of the Sudeten Germans mount steadily, and now his patience was exhausted. He would have the Sudetenland—or go to war. At the end of Hitler's tirade, Goebbels stepped to the microphone and shouted, "1918 will never be repeated!" Hitler, with a wild look in his eyes, slammed his fist on the lectern, cried "*Ja!*" and collapsed in his chair.

Chamberlain, dismayed by Hitler's half-mad speech, went on the radio to appeal for a diplomatic solution. On the air, he lamented the "horrible, fantastic, incredible" fact that "we should be digging trenches and trying on gas masks here because of a quarrel in a far-away country between peoples of whom we know nothing." Just hours before Hitler's new invasion deadline—two o'clock on September 28—Chamberlain sent an urgent message to Mussolini asking him to intercede. Chamberlain's plea arrived in Rome at about the same time as an American request from President Franklin Roosevelt that Mussolini urge Hitler to solve the dispute by international conference. Mussolini, too, was concerned, because he knew his armed forces were in no condition to fight and that he might be drawn into a world war. He called his ambassador in Berlin, Bernardo Attolico, who hurried to the Reich Chancellery.

The French ambassador, André François-Poncet, was already there, with a proposal to force immediate Czech evacuation of the Sudetenland. The scene at the Reich Chancellery that morning was chaotic. SS and Wehrmacht officers milled about, and waiters hurried to set tables for a luncheon of the commanders of the invasion units. François-Poncet found Hitler agitated and tense. While the ambassador was explaining the French proposal, an aide announced that Attolico had arrived with an urgent message from Mussolini. Hitler excused himself. In a neighboring salon, Attolico delivered Mussolini's plea for a postponement. Hitler hesitated only briefly. "Tell the duce that I accept," he said. A few minutes later,

On September 24, citizens of Prague take time to read newspapers headlined, "Mobilization" and "We Stand United."

A Lonely Mobilization

Determined to buck the odds and resist invasion, Czechs energetically prepared for war as the crisis with Germany deepened in late September 1938. In Prague and other cities, civilians staged air-raid drills, dug trenches, strapped on gas masks, and evacuated women and children to the countryside.

At the same time, more than a million reservists took up arms and reported to mobilization centers. "Their confidence is sometimes incredible," marveled an American correspondent there. "The Czechs would rather fight alone than lose part of their land without a fight."

Carrying their gas masks in tin canisters, women wait with their luggage and a pet dog at Prague's main railroad station for evacuation to the country.

Two men dig a trench, V-shaped against bomb blasts, in a field overlooked by Prague's ancient royal palace and the spires of Saint Vitus Cathedral.

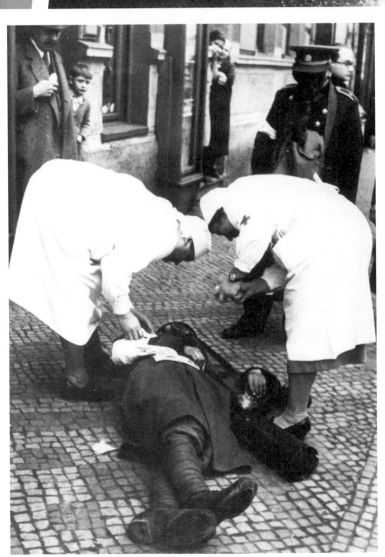

To make their air-raid drills as realistic as possible, Prague's civil-defense forces explode a dummy bomb in a downtown intersection (*above*). The sign on the street reads, "Target of the falling bomb." Officials also scattered simulated casualties in the city; at left, two nurses, observed by a warden in a gas mask, tend to a soldier-victim.

Grinning cockily, Czech reservists climb aboard a train heading for the frontier—and the war with Germany that never came.

Ambassador Henderson arrived with a proposal from Chamberlain for a summit conference of the concerned powers. Hitler accepted this suggestion, too, after making sure that Mussolini would attend the conference.

Why Hitler suddenly abandoned his invasion plan is not clear. He may have been influenced by the cautionary voices of his own generals and diplomats and particularly by warnings from his lieutenants Göring and Goebbels, neither of whom thought Germany was ready for war. Both Hungary and Poland were willing to apply pressure on Czechoslovakia, but neither was prepared to join Hitler's invasion. Now his most trusted ally, Mussolini, was also counseling restraint. Partial mobilization by the British and French had shown that their resolve was hardening. Moreover, Hitler could not have been encouraged by the apathy that he had witnessed the previous day. Standing on the Reich Chancellery balcony, he had reviewed a motorized division as it rumbled through Berlin. Few people on the street watched the procession, and those who did observed in silence, unable to summon a shred of enthusiasm for troops going off to another war.

Whatever his reasons, Hitler asked the leaders of France, Britain, and Italy to meet in Munich on September 29. Conspicuously, he omitted the leaders of Czechoslovakia. As the invitations were relayed to the capitals, a wave of relief swept western Europe. The mood in Paris, Ambassador Bullitt reported, could only be compared to the "feeling of relief when the news came that the armistice had been signed." In Berlin, when François-Poncet reported that Daladier would come to Munich, Göring cried, "Thank God!"

In London, Chamberlain was addressing the House of Commons about the crisis. In the galleries were the Queen Mother and other royalty, members of the high clergy, and many ambassadors. When the prime minister paused at the end of his speech, a note was thrust into his hand. He read it and turned again to the audience. "That is not all," he said. "I have something further to say to the House. I have now been informed by Herr Hitler that he invites me to meet him at Munich tomorrow morning. He has also invited Signor Mussolini and Monsieur Daladier. Signor Mussolini has accepted, and I have no doubt Monsieur Daladier will also accept. I need not say what my answer will be." Cheers broke out, and the House rose in applause.

The big decisions about Czechoslovakia, however, had already been made, and the statesmen who went to Munich were concerned only with ratifying them. Beneš suspected as much and sent a plea to Chamberlain for a Czech representative to be present so that "nothing may be done in Munich without Czechoslovakia being heard." Chamberlain promised only to "bear the point in mind." He knew well that Hitler controlled the conference and decided who would participate.

Mussolini arrived first, accompanied by Hitler, who had gone in his private train to meet the duce at Kiefersfelden on the old Austro-German boundary. Mussolini brought a list of German demands of Czechoslovakia that the Reich's Foreign Office had roughed out and dispatched to Rome. Hitler was not interested in talking about the demands, however. Instead, he harangued Mussolini about the war that the two of them must soon wage against France and England.

Chamberlain arrived in a buoyant mood. On the eve of his departure, he had received a two-word cable from President Roosevelt saying, "Good man," and he had told a cheering crowd at 10 Downing Street that they could go home and sleep quietly: "It will be all right now." Another happy throng waited at Munich's Regina Palace Hotel, where a band serenaded him with "Doing the Lambeth Walk."

Meanwhile, François-Poncet met Daladier, who descended from his plane looking "gloomy and preoccupied." At the Four Seasons Hotel, he briefly addressed the members of his delegation. "Everything depends on the English," said Daladier. "We can do nothing but follow them."

Shortly after noon, the principals assembled at the Führerhaus, an ugly concrete building that served as Nazi party headquarters. Hitler, looking pale and tense, received his guests in a salon upstairs, where a buffet luncheon was being served. Daladier had never met the Führer, and his first impression was disquieting: "His dull blue eyes, shifting rapidly during the brief greetings, gave him a hard and remote expression. He was dressed very simply, like a man of the people, in a khaki jacket, with a swastika armband on the right sleeve and long trousers falling on scuffed black shoes." Daladier judged him capable of anything.

Hitler had no interest in the buffet, so the principals and selected aides— eight or nine people in all—adjourned to his office. The conference had been organized so hastily that there was no agenda, no seating plan, no pads and pencils on the table or ink in the inkwells. Hitler thanked his guests for coming and then recited the now-familiar crimes of the Czechs. He gruffly brushed aside Chamberlain's request that a Czech representative be present, and Chamberlain did not insist. The discussion wandered until Mussolini retrieved from his pocket the memorandum the Germans had sent to him in Rome the previous afternoon. He now presented the list of demands as his own concoction. When it was translated, Chamberlain and Daladier agreed that the document merited discussion. In doing so, they effectively renounced any serious effort to oppose Hitler's designs on Czechoslovakia. Although they did not know that the memorandum had originated in the German Foreign Office, they quickly realized that the demands were exactly what the Führer required.

The Munich Agreement of September 29, 1938, bears signatures scrawled by four European heads of government: France's Daladier, Italy's Mussolini, Great Britain's Chamberlain, and Germany's Hitler. In the picture at far right, the duce confers with Hermann Göring as Hitler bends over to sign the document, which gave Germany the Czech Sudetenland. It was, the Führer promised, "the last territorial claim I have to make in Europe."

Geheime Reichssache

Abkommen

zwischen Deutschland, dem Vereinigten Königreich,
Frankreich und Italien,
getroffen in München, am 29. September 1938.

Deutschland, das Vereinigte Königreich,
Frankreich und Italien sind unter Berücksichtigung
des Abkommens, das hinsichtlich der Abtretung des
sudetendeutschen Gebiets bereits grundsätzlich er-
zielt wurde, über folgende Bedingungen und Modali-
täten dieser ... ... kommen und erklären
... ... teln verantwortlich
... ... füllung notwendigen

— 4 —

7.) Es wird ein Optionsrecht für den Übertritt in
die abgetretenen Gebiete und für den Austritt aus
ihnen vorgesehen. Die Option muss innerhalb von
sechs Monaten vom Zeitpunkt des Abschlusses dieses
Abkommens an ausgeübt werden. Ein deutsch-tsche-
choslowakischer Ausschuss wird die Einzelheiten der
Option bestimmen, Verfahren zur Erleichterung des
Austausches der Bevölkerung erwägen und grundsätzli-
che Fragen klären, die sich aus diesem Austausch
ergeben.

... ... ber.
... ... nkreich und Italien
... ... blets bis zum
... ... hne Zerstörung
... ... en, und dass
... ... Verantwortung
... ... hädigung der
... ... wird.

8.) Die Tschechoslowakische Regierung wird innerhalb
einer Frist von vier Wochen vom Tage des Abschlusses dieses Abkommens an alle Sudetendeutschen aus
ihren militärischen und polizeilichen Verbänden entlassen, die diese Entlassung wünschen. Innerhalb
derselben Frist wird die Tschechoslowakische Regierung
sudetendeutsche Gefangene entlassen, die wegen poli-
tischer Delikte Freiheitsstrafen verbüssen.

München, den 29. September 1938.

Mussolini Adolf Hitler Édouard Daladier Neville Chamberlain

8.)

Nothing remained for the principals to do but work out the details of the Czech concession. As the afternoon wore on, ambassadors, officials, and adjutants slipped into Hitler's office and ranged themselves around the walls. Aides and secretaries came and went as new versions and translations of the Mussolini memorandum were produced and passed back and forth. Fascist Black Shirts and young SS officers filled the corridors. Göring was much in evidence; François-Poncet thought Göring's white uniform "accentuated his curves." Mussolini was the only one at the conference table who seemed to enjoy himself. Daladier appeared gloomy and bitter, Chamberlain harassed and preoccupied. Hitler sat on a sofa crossing and recrossing his legs and occasionally holding his watch as if his patience had reached an end. As the evening passed, a state banquet for the delegations had to be canceled. At last, early on the morning of September 30, the Munich Agreement was typed in four languages and signed by the four heads of state. His demands met but cheated out of war, Hitler angrily scratched his signature, noted a British diplomat, "as if he were being asked to sign away his birthright."

The document was short. Its preamble acknowledged that cession of the Sudetenland had been agreed on and that what followed addressed "terms and conditions." In fact, Hitler had already laid out the terms and even the timetable—evacuation of the Sudetenland October 1-10. Now, an international commission of representatives from Germany, Britain, France, Italy, and Czechoslovakia was proposed to oversee the evacuation. The commission would also determine the final location of frontiers. An annex to the agreement stated that if the problems of Polish and Hungarian minorities in Czechoslovakia had not been settled in three months, the heads of the four powers would meet again. In another annex, Britain and France guaranteed Czechoslovakia's new boundaries, and Germany and Italy promised to do so as soon as Polish and Hungarian claims had been settled.

Behind the verbiage was the stark fact that the Munich Agreement had crippled the country of Czechoslovakia. The Czechs lost their frontier fortifications and much of their network of railroads, along with most of their steel, chemical, textile, coal, and electric-power industries. In the 16,000 square miles of territory they ceded stood important timber reserves. Czechoslovakia relinquished to the Reich not only 3.5 million Sudeten

Germans, but hundreds of thousands of citizens of Czech and Slovak origin.

After all the copies had been signed and Hitler had thanked the participants, the British and French had the unpleasant duty of bearing the bitter news to the Czechs. On the afternoon of the conference, Hubert Masařík of the Czech Foreign Ministry and Vojtéch Mastný, the Czech minister in Berlin, had arrived in Munich as observers attached to the British delegation. They had been met at the airport like "police suspects," Masařík recalled. Accompanied by Gestapo agents, they had been taken in a police car to the Regina Palace Hotel and confined to their rooms with a guard at the door. At quarter past two the next morning, Chamberlain and Daladier met them in Chamberlain's room and gave them a copy of the agreement. Mastný, who read it aloud, shed tears. When Masařík asked if a response from his government was expected, he was told that no time remained for discussion because the first stage of German occupation would begin the next day.

Indeed, when Prague received a copy of the Munich text at 6:20 a.m., it was clear that nothing more could be said or done. Czechoslovakia's choice, remarked Premier Jan Syrový bitterly, was "between being murdered and committing suicide." After the government made the decision to capitulate, six senior generals headed by the chief of the general staff called on Beneš to ask him to reconsider. Now was the right time to fight, they said. The army had mobilized 1.25 million troops to oppose the thirty-seven divisions the Germans had massed on the frontier. The nation could certainly hold out for several months, and by then the Western powers would be shamed

At left, in their home ten miles from the German frontier, a Sudeten family makes a string of pro-German pennants to welcome Hitler's occupying troops. Below, as German soldiers march through the border town of Asch, youngsters wearing peasant costumes join the triumphant parade.

into coming to its aid. But Beneš lacked faith in England and France. He sadly turned his generals down. That evening, in an address to the nation, Syrový announced, "We are deserted, and we stand alone. We had the choice between a desperate and hopeless defense and acceptance of conditions unparalleled in history for ruthlessness." On October 1, German troops marched into the Sudetenland.

The signatories to the agreement, meanwhile, returned home to almost-universal acclaim. Chamberlain lingered in Munich long enough to arrange a private audience with Hitler at the Führer's apartment. There he prevailed on Hitler to sign a short statement of Anglo-German friendship that proclaimed the two peoples' desire to reconcile any future differences by consultation rather than war. Highly pleased with himself, Chamberlain then departed for England, where crowds lining his route from the airport greeted him with frenzied cheers. At Buckingham Palace, he received the thanks of the king. He told a throng outside 10 Downing Street that he had brought back "peace with honor" and believed it to be "peace for our time."

Daladier, too, was greeted at the airport by crowds shouting, *La paix!* Women ran to him holding their babies for him to touch. Towns throughout France would change the names of their principal streets to Avenue Édouard Daladier. A similar reception awaited Mussolini. He walked with Hitler to the Munich railroad station through crowds chanting, "Führer! Duce!" When he returned to Rome, he passed triumphantly through a facsimile of the Arch of Constantine.

Yet amid the chorus of international acclaim there were notes of dissent. An impassioned Winston Churchill pronounced Munich a "disaster of the first magnitude" and predicted that it was "only the beginning of the reckoning." In France, Daladier himself referred privately to Munich as the "terrible day." When his plane descended

Father Josef Tiso, a Catholic priest and Slovak nationalist, emerged from the disintegration of Czechoslovakia as the premier of a new Nazi puppet state, the Republic of Slovakia. Hitler gave Tiso a choice: throw in with Nazi Germany or see Slovakia fed to Poland and Hungary.

Magyar peasants in Ruthenia, the easternmost province of Czechoslovakia, welcome as liberators the Hungarian troops who occupied their lands. The ecstatic man in the foreground holds aloft a portrait of Nicholas Horthy, the Hungarian regent and hero of the Great War.

for a landing at Paris, he saw the crowds below and thought at first they were there to attack him. When he realized that he was wrong, Daladier snapped, "Idiots! They do not know what they applaud."

Prominent among the dissenters was Adolf Hitler. Far from regarding Munich as a triumph, he believed it to be a disaster. The agreement had deprived him of the war he wanted, and he would come to think of the episode as the greatest mistake of his career. To the end of his life, he would regret that Chamberlain had caused him to start his war a year too late. "We ought to have gone to war in 1938," he said in his Berlin bunker in February 1945. "September 1938 would have been the most favorable date."

No matter how the leaders felt about Munich, it soon became clear that the agreement had not brought "peace for our time" as Chamberlain had promised. The international commission appointed to work out details of the German occupation discovered quickly that it had no real power. The German generals achieved the border they wanted after Ribbentrop bluntly explained that they would establish the frontier by force if necessary. The idea of holding plebiscites to determine the wishes of the populations involved was abandoned. When François-Poncet attempted a compromise more responsive to the wishes of the Czechs, he was denounced by Ribbentrop and reminded by his own government that he must "do nothing to spoil the effects of Munich."

In the middle of October, Hitler asked his generals to prepare plans for the final liquidation of Czechoslovakia. In the meantime, he pursued his

As stunned citizens of Prague look on, a German motorcycle unit crosses the Charles Bridge on the Moldau River. The only resistance to the German seizure of the city was a few snowballs hurled at the troops.

familiar tactic of dismantling the Czech state from within. When Hungary and Czechoslovakia could not agree on a new border, Hitler dictated a new eastern frontier that made more than a million Slovaks and Ruthenians citizens of Hungary. At the same time, Germany encouraged what remained of the provinces of Slovakia and Ruthenia to demand almost-total autonomy. The German Propaganda Ministry mounted a campaign accusing the Prague government of terrorizing the Slovak minority. German agents in Slovakia recruited radical Slovak nationalists to fuel disorder so that Hitler could justify a German occupation as the only alternative to anarchy. Exhausted by the Munich crisis and the growing unrest in his country, President Beneš had resigned under German threats on October 5 and gone into exile in England. He had been replaced by Emil Hácha, a sixty-six-year-old jurist who suffered from a heart condition and by his own admission knew nothing of politics. In an attempt to restore order to his rapidly disintegrating country, Hácha began talks with Slovak nationalist leaders. When this effort failed, he played into Hitler's hands by jailing leading Slovak separatists and dismissing the Slovak prime minister, Josef Tiso. The Germans responded by applying so much pressure on the Slo-

vakian parliament that its members voted unanimously for independence.

On March 14, the demoralized and ailing Hácha asked to see Hitler. He was received at quarter past one the following morning, an hour that Hitler chose deliberately to ensure that Hácha's resistance would be low. The Führer told Hácha that conditions in Czechoslovakia were so chaotic that he was obliged to send in German troops to restore order and establish a protectorate. The army would march at six o'clock. If Hácha would direct the Czech army and people not to resist, they would be guaranteed a certain amount of national liberty. Otherwise, Czechoslovakia would be mercilessly bombed and treated as a conquered state.

Hácha tried to bargain, but he was so harried by Hitler, Ribbentrop, and Göring that he twice fainted at the conference table and had to be given injections of stimulants by Hitler's personal physician. Finally, at four o'clock, he signed a document saying he "confidently placed the fate of the Czech people and country in the hands of the Führer of the German Reich." Hitler was now authorized to march. In another document prepared for his signature, Hácha ordered Czech troops to remain in their barracks and lay down their arms.

At about ten o'clock that morning, young George Kennan, who was serving as a political officer at the American embassy, saw the first German armor enter Prague in a driving snowstorm. "A crowd of embittered but curious Czechs looked on in silence," he wrote. "Many of the women were weeping into their handkerchiefs. For the rest of the day, the motorized units pounded and roared over the cobblestone streets; hundreds and hundreds of vehicles plastered with snow. By evening, the occupation was complete, and the people were chased off the streets by an eight o'clock curfew. It was strange to see these Prague streets, usually so animated, now completely empty." Independent Czechoslovakia had ceased to exist. ✠

Clenched fists and furious faces meet German motorized troops as they roll unopposed through Prague on March 15, 1939.

The domed Church of Saint Alexander dominates a mid-nineteenth-century neighborhood built when Warsaw was emerging as a major industrial city. The handsome apartment buildings flanking the church were homes for wealthy merchants and manufacturers.

A couple settles into a *dorozka* in front of the Saxon Palace, once the residence of Polish kings.

Last Days of a Proud City

Peacetime Warsaw challenged even Paris and Rome for breathtaking vistas and architectural treasures. Rising on a terrace above the Vistula River, it was an urban feast of treelined avenues and emerald parks, of shadowed medieval back streets and soaring steeples. The city dazzled visitors with its extravagantly ornamented palaces, and it boasted all the cultural trappings of municipal prosperity—fine museums, a great university, a splendid opera house.

Romantic charm was everywhere in evidence. Comfortable horse-drawn taxis called *dorozki* plied the avenues, farmers sold their produce in open markets, and artisans wove cloth and made shoes in the same streets that had once housed medieval craft guilds.

As the capital of a restored Polish state and a center for new automobile and aircraft industries, Warsaw doubled in population, to 1.35 million, in the two decades after the Great War. Through the fateful summer of 1939, native Varsovians sipping their morning coffee at tables along Ujazdowska Avenue had every reason to feel that the future was bright. Even those who noticed the ominous chill in Europe's political climate could take comfort—however short-lived—in their city's motto, *Contemnit procellas*—"It defies the storm."

Narrow four- and five-story houses dating from the sixteenth century rise above the Stare Miasto, or old town. It was here that the city's history began almost a thousand years ago.

Sisters of Charity, members of a religious community that operated one of the hospitals in the capital, cross the market square on their way to nearby Saint John's Cathedral. Prewar Warsaw was 75 percent Catholic.

A girl sits before an eighteenth-century house known for its bas-relief sailing vessel—a relic of the days when barges carried grain down the Vistula to Danzig for transshipment by sea to the ports of northern Europe.

Electric streetcars travel up Marszalkowska Street, the main commercial artery in the city. Furriers, dressmakers, jewelers, and a gourmet delicatessen located on the avenue catered to Warsaw's most affluent citizens.

Shoppers examine produce for sale on a cobbled back street. Each morning, vendors went to the Vistula River to load their pushcarts with foodstuffs and flowers brought on riverboats from farms in the provinces.

A Jewish shopkeeper peers from behind his eclectic wares—yarn, coat hangers, suspenders, and insoles. Warsaw's Jewish population of nearly 350,000 was the largest of any city in Europe.

Peasant women in plaid shawls mingle with their customers in a market set up amid workers' homes on the outskirts of the city. The enterprising women sold fruits, vegetables, sausages, cheese, and butter wrapped in green leaves to keep it fresh.

Lazienki Palace, built during the 1700s as the summer residence of King Stanisław August, was located in a public park where lovers met and families picnicked on Sundays after church.

An army corporal and his companion, whose hat marks her as a university student, stroll beneath the fragrant lime trees of Ujazdowska Avenue—known, because of its outdoor cafés, as the Champs Élysées of Warsaw.

Onslaught from the Air

Inside a darkened airdrome, Luftwaffe bomber crews sweating out the prelaunch hours on September 1, 1939, sensed they were about to make history. Their mission, a surprise attack on Polish warships and port facilities, was to be part of an unprecedented air assault. Its purpose was nothing less than to destroy in one massive blow a nation's capacity to defend itself.

As it turned out, capricious fortune in the shape of a blinding fog delayed the attack and cost the Germans their moment of surprise. Once the air cleared, hundreds of twin-engine Heinkel 111s and Dornier 17s roared over the Polish plain, demolishing airfields, smashing bridges, and terrorizing civilians. Scores of Stukas swept low in support of German tanks and infantry. But the Polish air force, alerted by now, dispersed its planes to auxiliary airstrips and rose to challenge the invaders. Polish aircraft and flak shot down more than seventy German bombers, whose defensive armament proved insufficient. The Luftwaffe, however, had an advantage in numbers, communications, and tactical planning; the scattered Polish squadrons could respond only in piecemeal, if heroic, fashion. Soon the

Luftwaffe controlled the skies. German dive bombers became flying artillery, swooping ahead of the advancing panzers to blast enemy strongpoints. The Heinkels and Dorniers, screened by fighter escorts, paralyzed the Polish armies, battering reinforcements, supplies, and ammunition before they could reach the front. The pictures here and on the following pages illustrate the performance of one of those units, Kampfgeschwader 1, which had been designated the Hindenburg Group in honor of Germany's World War I hero-general. As the emblem above indicates, the Hindenburgers specialized in bombing railroads. But all of Poland was their target, and they struck mercilessly everywhere—even at the heart of Warsaw. After the campaign, these photographs were included in an album given as a memento of victory to the Führer.

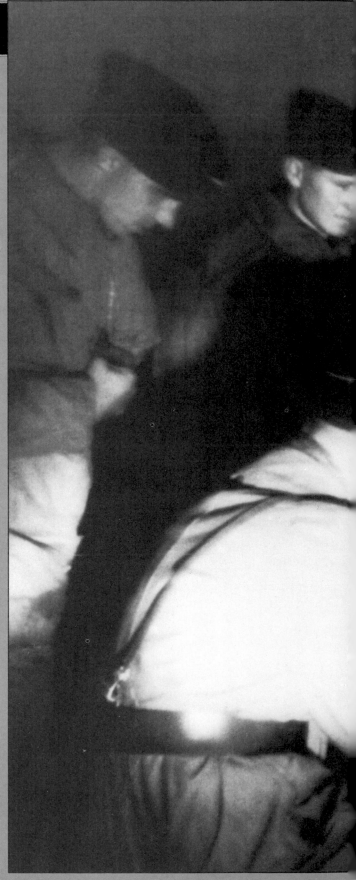

Absorbed in a card game called skat, aviators of **Kampfge-**

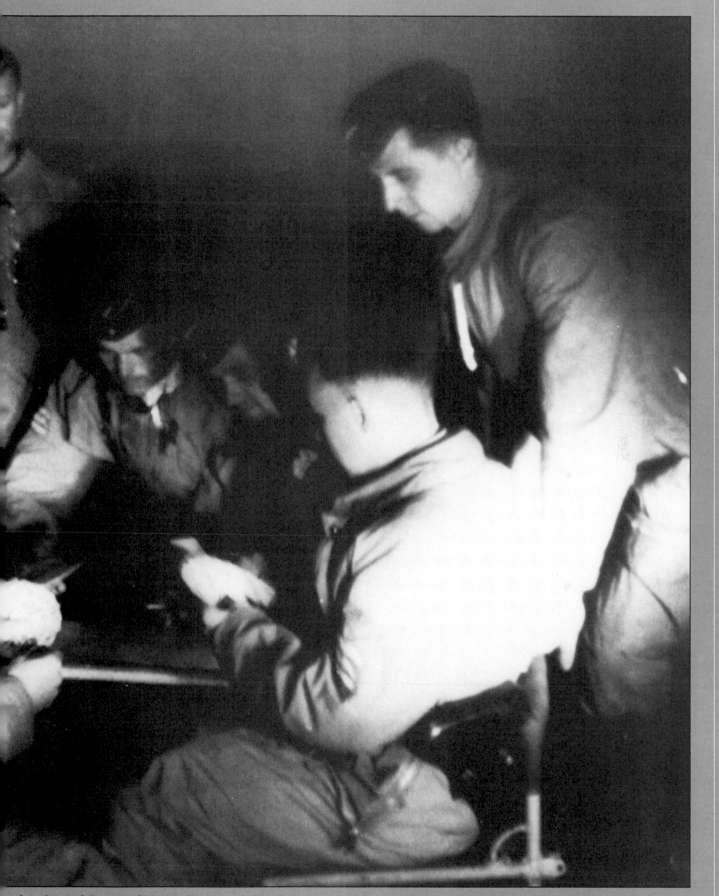

schwader 1 while away the prestrike hours before dawn on September 1 at their base near Kolberg on the Baltic coast.

Members of the Hindenburg Group's ground crew load ammunition into drum magazines used by the three 7.92-mm machine guns on their Heinkel bombers. The defensive weaponry was inadequate against even lightly armed Polish planes.

Another crewman stacks 2.2-pound incendiaries before loading them into an He 111. The Luftwaffe's medium-range bombers dropped thousands of these thermite and magnesium firebombs, which burst into intense flames when they hit the ground.

Hauling hoses onto the wings, a ground crew fills the main tanks of an He 111E with high-octane fuel. Fast refueling enabled the group to fly three or more raids a day from the base at Kolberg.

Stripped to their shorts in the late-summer heat, two armorers winch 110-pound high-explosive bombs into a Heinkel's bomb bay. These general-purpose bombs were used to destroy buildings, rip up railroad tracks, and blast craters in roads.

Over enemy territory, a Heinkel's bombardier-navigator, in a criss-cross parachute harness, clearly views a Polish town through the plane's glass-enclosed nose.

A pilot sits at the controls, which were above and behind the bombardier's perch but in the same glassed-in forward area.

Watching intently for any Polish PZL-P.11 fighters that might have gotten off the ground, a belly gunner sights the single machine gun mounted in a gondola on the plane's underside.

With pencils, a chart, and a compass arrayed on his lap, the bombardier-navigator plots the Heinkel's course to a target in Poland. When not operating the bombsight, the navigator sat in a seat next to the pilot's.

⊲ Viewed through the spinning propeller of one bomber, a second Heinkel laden with incendiary bombs flies toward a target in the lake-strewn countryside of northern Poland.

Explosives delivered by Heinkels ranging deep into Poland have blasted a bridge over the Bug River, choking off a critical supply route from the east.

⊲ A stick of bombs plunges earth-ward, aimed at a strategic road that cuts through farmland behind the front. Bombs dropped by the mission's lead aircraft can be seen exploding below.

Gas-storage tanks near Warsaw erupt in smoke after a low-level bombing run. The Luftwaffe restricted its bombing of the heavily populated capital to such strategic targets until Polish troops, retreating into the city, fortified its streets and buildings.

Fires raging on both sides of the Vistula River in Warsaw fill the sky with smoke. Massive incendiary raids in late September burned entire districts, adding the threat of fire to the trials of Warsaw's beleaguered defenders.

FOUR

The Armies Unleashed

The summons would have seized the attention of any European diplomat in the fall of 1938. Joachim von Ribbentrop, Hitler's heavy-handed foreign minister, desired the company of the Polish ambassador to Germany, Josef Lipski, at lunch in Berchtesgaden's Grand Hotel on October 24. Given the stunning events that had followed Ribbentrop's recent conversations with representatives of Austria and Czechoslovakia, and considering that Prussia and other neighbors had erased Poland from the map of Europe for more than a century—until the Allied powers re-created the nation at the Versailles conference in 1919—the invitation must have set the Polish envoy's thoughts whirling.

Yet Ambassador Lipski had reason to believe that there was little to fear. Relations with Germany had never been warmer. Poland's ten-year non-aggression pact with Nazi Germany was in only its fourth year, and Poland still enjoyed most-favored-nation status as part of a recent trade agreement. Moreover, Hitler had publicly stated that the annexation of the Sudetenland, accomplished at the Munich conference less than a month earlier, had satisfied his "last territorial claim" in Europe.

Contemplating Ribbentrop's invitation, Lipski and his foreign minister, Józef Beck, may well have seen an opportunity to push their own goals for Poland. Since neither France nor Great Britain seemed inclined to oppose Germany's aggressive actions in central Europe, the Polish leaders decided to act independently in order to gain whatever diplomatic and territorial concessions they could. In the back of Beck's mind was a grand design for a so-called Third Europe, an alliance of Baltic and Balkan countries that might offer collective safety from Nazi or Soviet aggression. The forty-four-year-old Beck, an aloof, unpleasant man, was part of a junta of three former colonels who had assumed control of the Polish government after the death in 1935 of modern Poland's first president, the legendary Marshal Józef Pilsudski. While President Ignacy Mościcki held political power and Marshal Edward Rydz-Smigly commanded the armed forces, Beck had full authority in foreign affairs. Under his leadership, Poland had taken advantage of Germany's point-of-the-bayonet diplomacy to settle old scores.

An armored column of the 4th Panzer Division crosses the shallow Bzura River, forty miles west of Warsaw, on September 16, 1939. The unseasonably dry weather favored the invaders, because it made the rivers fordable and the ground firm enough for heavy vehicles.

135

Three days after the German Anschluss with Austria, Beck issued an ultimatum to Lithuania, threatening war unless Lithuania agreed to establish diplomatic and trade relations within forty-eight hours. His goal was a nonaligned bloc consisting of Poland, the Baltic republics, and the Scandinavian states. Although Poland and Lithuania had historic ties that stretched back hundreds of years, problems between the two nations had arisen in 1919, when Poland and the new communist regime in Russia began a bloody six-month war over their common border. After the Red Army had captured Vilna, a Lithuanian city populated largely by ethnic Poles (it was also Pilsudski's birthplace), the Polish army attacked, driving out the Soviets. But when Lithuania attempted to reclaim the city, the Poles refused to leave. Militarily weak, Lithuania retaliated as harshly as it could—by severing not only diplomatic relations, but all telegraph lines, railroad tracks, and roads connecting the two countries. For nearly twenty years, it had refused even to hold talks with Poland.

The Polish maneuver caught Hitler off balance, but only for a moment. He ordered the German high command to make plans for an advance into Lithuania, should it and Poland go to war. The Führer's objective was to seize the ice-free Baltic port of Memel and as much Lithuanian territory as possible. Meanwhile, Lithuania's leaders desperately sought international support to ward off the Polish threat, but the Great Powers were preoccupied with Nazi Germany. The Lithuanians found themselves isolated and had no choice but to yield.

When Hitler went after Czechoslovakia, Beck imitated his bullying tactics against its troubled leaders. While Hitler escalated his demands for the annexation of the Sudetenland, Poland similarly demanded the return of Teschen, a 400-square-mile, coal-rich industrial region that Czechoslovakia had won from Poland in 1920, when the boundaries of the two nations were dictated by the Allies.

Throughout the worsening crisis, Poland kept pace with Hitler, insisting that the ethnic Poles of Teschen be granted the same rights as the Germans in the Sudetenland. And although Poland failed to push its way into the Munich conference, it won an identical victory. On September 30, 1938, the Poles demanded that Czechoslovak forces immediately evacuate Teschen. The government in Prague complied, and the next day Polish troops marched into the territory as the Nazis occupied the Sudetenland.

Poland's coup earned the Warsaw government no friends in the West. The president of the United States, Franklin D. Roosevelt, remarked that the Teschen affair reminded him of a schoolyard fight between a big boy and a little boy. While the big boy held the little boy on the ground, Roosevelt said, "a third boy stepped forward and kicked the little boy in the stomach."

German citizens of Memel, the Baltic port ceded to Lithuania under the Versailles treaty, campaign for the pro-Nazi United Front of German Parties during a legislative election in 1935.

Hermann Göring, on the other hand, expressed admiration for the grab of Teschen, calling it a "very bold action, performed in excellent style." Few heeded the bitter comment of the Czech general who delivered the district to the advancing Polish army. Before long, he warned, the Poles themselves would be handing the region to the Germans.

No such prospect would have seemed credible to Ambassador Lipski as he drove to the Grand Hotel on that October day. Ribbentrop greeted him warmly, and the lunch began well. But before long, the German foreign minister came to the point. He had three proposals to make regarding a "general settlement of the issues between Poland and Germany."

First, said Ribbentrop, the Baltic seaport of Danzig, known to the Poles as Gdansk, must be returned to Germany. When the victors of the world war re-created the state of Poland, they awarded the Poles a strip of land running along the Vistula River to the Baltic Sea in order to prevent the country from being landlocked. The Polish Corridor, as the area was known, severed Germany from its province of East Prussia. Although Danzig, at the northern end of the corridor, was populated largely by Germans, it was declared a free city, democratically governed under the supervision of a high commissioner appointed by the League of Nations. The city was demilitarized and shared customs, port authority, and other administrative operations with the Poles, who were given responsibility for Danzig's protection and its foreign policy.

The decision outraged Germans of all political stripes, and Danzig became a perpetual irritant between the two countries. The clamor increased in the early 1930s, when Nazis gained a majority in the city government. President Pilsudski warned his fellow Poles that Germany would reveal its true intentions toward Poland by what it tried to do with Danzig.

Ribbentrop's second proposal concerned the corridor proper. Under the terms of Versailles, Poland could not bar German passage to East Prussia but could extract transit payments for commercial shipments. Germany, to end this drain on its foreign-exchange credits, now insisted on building a highway and railroad system through the corridor, for which it required extraterritorial status.

The foreign minister cloaked his third proposal in a response to something the Poles themselves had requested—an extension of the 1934 non-aggression agreement. Germany would renew it for an additional twenty-five years, but on one condition: Poland must sign the Anti-Comintern Pact, which Germany and Japan had concluded in November 1936 to express their opposition to the spread of communism. Ever since the Third Communist International, or Comintern—a conference held in Paris in 1919—the worldwide communist movement, centered in Moscow, had espoused the overthrow of all noncommunist governments.

Although the Poles were staunchly anticommunist, they could not accept this demand. Poland's major foreign-policy goal was to maintain a balance between its two giant neighbors. Poland had signed a nonaggression pact with the Soviets, just as it had with the Nazis. Now Germany was demanding that Poland choose sides. To concur would be an act of submission that would perilously tilt the Polish position.

For three hours the two diplomats talked. At last, a shaken Lipski left, only to be summoned back to the hotel a half-hour later. Ribbentrop presented a new idea. The troubles with Czechoslovakia might lead to war, he said. If Poland came in on the German side, the Germans would make it worthwhile: Should Poland desire a common border with Hungary, Germany would grant it. Ruthenia could be detached from Czechoslovakia and annexed by the Hungarians, and Slovakia could be detached and apportioned to Poland as a client state.

The German assured Lipski there was no hurry for answers, but the Polish ambassador knew better. He caught the first train to Warsaw and reported to Beck. Both men recognized at once that Poland faced a crisis, but neither grasped its full gravity. Speaking for Hitler, Ribbentrop had in fact pronounced a death sentence on the country's freedom, if not its very existence. So far, the Führer had been pleased with Poland's synchronistic policies, but he could not tolerate the Poles' unpredictable independence. He was determined to secure his eastern borders, whatever the price, but he was prepared to give the Poles a few months' grace while he dismantled Czechoslovakia. Then Poland would either have to demonstrate its subservience or be subdued by force.

Although Beck could sense the looming specter of war, he felt there was still a chance to cut a deal with Germany. But he harbored several illusions. For one thing, he believed that the German proposals were simply trial balloons floated by the Nazi foreign minister, not critical tenets of Hitler's policy. For another, Beck believed that Germany might value a strong, sympathetic Poland as an eastern buffer to the Soviet Union. These assumptions led Beck to conclude that Germany could be checkmated diplomatically, especially if Poland and the Western Allies stood together. He sent Lipski back to Berlin with a response to the first of Ribbentrop's points: Poland would not give up Danzig, and any attempt by Germany to take it "must inevitably lead to a conflict." Poland would, however, be willing to start negotiations on a new Danzig treaty, one that would ease tensions and exclude the League of Nations.

Wise in the ways of intimidation, Ribbentrop allowed the Polish ambassador to cool his heels for two weeks before granting him an audience. Then he summarily dismissed the Danzig issue with a comment about the need for head-to-head talks with Beck. Lipski and Beck nervously pondered Poland's next move for a few weeks. Then they decided to invite Ribbentrop to Warsaw. The Germans countered by suggesting that Beck come to Germany and meet with Hitler himself, and on January 5, 1939, Beck made the same climb to the mountaintop at Berchtesgaden that Austria's chancellor, Kurt von Schuschnigg, had made the previous February. But Beck was not treated as brutally as Schuschnigg. This time, the Führer made no threats and set no deadlines. Neither did he yield an inch. "Danzig," Hitler declared, "is German and will remain German and will sooner or later become part of Germany." But for now, the Führer dangled the bait for Poland's submission to German dominance. The rump state of Czechoslovakia must be disposed of, he said. By cooperating in its demise, Poland could reap the benefits of a German-guaranteed western border and more territory from Slovakia.

Beck came away truly alarmed. The points Ribbentrop had made were actually Hitler's demands. He hurried back to Warsaw and warned his government to prepare for the possibility of war. Hitler, for his part, left the meeting convinced that it would take more than diplomatic arm-twisting to subdue the stubborn, fiercely independent Poles.

The Führer then tightened the screws. On March 15, he completed the dismemberment of Czechoslovakia without bothering to notify Poland. Slovakia, the promised prize, became a German satellite. On March 21, Ribbentrop called in Lipski and delivered a tongue-lashing. By this time, German forces had access to several hundred additional miles of Poland's southern border. The Polish response to the German proposals had been so unsatisfactory, the foreign minister declared, that the Führer had begun to doubt Poland's sincerity.

That same day, Hitler moved against Lithuania. Like Poland, Lithuania possessed a single seaport, Memel, which had been acquired from Germany under the Versailles treaty and was a prime Nazi target. Hitler had

On the snowy steps of the Berghof, his mountain retreat, Hitler *(back to camera)* welcomes the Polish foreign minister, Józef Beck, on January 5, 1939. In the meeting that followed, Hitler demanded the return of Danzig and a right of way through the Polish Corridor to East Prussia.

long since taken the preliminary steps to undermine the Lithuanian position there, organizing a vocal Nazi minority to call for reunion with Germany. He had delayed more overt action until he could settle his dispute with Poland. Now, with hopes of Polish acquiescence dimming, Hitler turned on Lithuania and demanded the immediate surrender of its port. Lithuania capitulated on March 23.

The day after the German occupation of Memel, Beck summoned his senior diplomats to a meeting in Warsaw. Lipski, in despair, offered to resign his ambassadorship so that someone else could try to salvage Polish sovereignty, but Beck refused to hear of it. He was still prepared to negotiate with the Nazis. But not at any price. Poland, he said, would not "join that category of eastern states that allow rules to be dictated to them." If Poland's independence is challenged, Beck said, "we will fight." Nor was the foreign minister prepared to admit that the cause was hopeless. Beck assured the Poles, "We have arrived at this difficult moment in our politics with all the trump cards in our hand."

The idea that Poland held any cards at all seemed unrealistic—until an electrifying announcement was made in London one week later. On March 31, Prime Minister Neville Chamberlain, speaking for both England and France, declared in the House of Commons that the two nations had at last drawn a line in the dirt. "In the event of any action which clearly threatened Polish independence, and which the Polish government considered it vital to resist with their national forces," he stated, both countries were prepared to assist the Poles.

Chamberlain's decision infuriated Hitler. "I'll cook a stew that they'll choke on," he fumed to Admiral Wilhelm Canaris, the counterintelligence chief of the German high command. The following day, Hitler used the launching of the battleship *Tirpitz* to lash out at England. "If anyone should wish to pit his strength against ours with violence," he thundered, "the German people will accept the challenge."

In the rush to contain the Nazi menace, both the British and the French had discounted the Soviet Union, largely because everyone assumed that the ideological gap between the communists and fascists was so great that Josef Stalin would automatically side with any anti-Hitler camp. After Stalin's recent purges of his top military commanders, however, it seemed unlikely that the Red Army, despite its vast size, was in any condition to take the field. Chamberlain, moreover, despised the Russians. But the strategic advantages of an alliance with them were now so great that Chamberlain belatedly opened negotiations with Moscow. His hope was to forge a treaty allying Great Britain, France, and Russia against further German aggression and guaranteeing the safety of several east European countries, including Poland. The Poles, however, regarded with open hostility the hand extended to Moscow and were horrified at the prospect of the Red Army entering their territory.

Hitler, meanwhile, continued his war of nerves, posing as a peace-loving statesman while secretly preparing for war. "The chief impression which I had of Hitler," wrote Sir Nevile Henderson, the British ambassador to Berlin, "was that of a master chess player studying the board and waiting for his opponent to make some false move." On April 3, three days after Britain's announcement of solidarity with Poland, the Führer issued Case White, a top-secret directive to the German armed forces. It required the preparation of detailed plans for an invasion of Poland, to be ready for execution by September 1, 1939. Hitler was determined to avoid negotiations. He felt that when the Western powers had granted his demands at Munich, they had boxed him in, limiting his success to his basic demands. He had wanted a war over Czechoslovakia, and now he was determined to have one over Poland.

Three days after the distribution of Case White, Lipski was summoned to the German Foreign Office. This time there was no lunch. The ambassador was informed that Germany's terms for settlement of the issues between the two nations were no longer negotiable.

Europe caught the jitters at the prospect of a German-Polish war. Tensions increased on April 7, when the Italians invaded Albania. In response, Great Britain and France sent pledges of support to Greece and Rumania, and President Roosevelt dispatched letters to Hitler and Mussolini asking the two dictators to give assurances that they would not attack any of a long list of nations—thirty-one in all. Poland was among them.

On April 28, Hitler replied in a speech to the Reichstag that was broadcast around the world. After claiming that the German representatives at Versailles "were subjected to even greater degradations than can ever have been inflicted on the chieftains of the Sioux tribes," he ridiculed Roosevelt's concerns point by point. Reports of German plans to attack Poland, he said, were "inventions of the international press." All that Germany wanted was a peaceful accord on the basis of mutual respect. Then he denounced the 1935 Anglo-German Naval Agreement and declared that the German-Polish nonaggression declaration of 1934 had been "infringed by Poland and thereby was no longer in existence." The Reichstag endorsed Hitler's decision with thunderous applause.

The Poles still hoped for a compromise. In early May, Beck responded to Hitler with a firm speech of his own. Poland would not yield to German bullying, he said: "We in Poland do not recognize the concept of peace at

German refugees from Poland cross a railroad trestle into Germany. Even as Hitler assailed the alleged mistreatment of ethnic Germans in foreign countries, he deprived Jews living in Germany of their rights simply because they were Jewish.

any price. There is only one thing in the life of men, nations, and states that is without price, and this is honor."

Through late spring and early summer, Beck worked to augment his government's understandings with England and France. The French promised to attack Germany by air at the outbreak of war, conduct a diversionary ground attack three days later, and launch a full-scale invasion within fifteen days. England was less specific, talking of bombing attacks by the Royal Air Force and the possibility of sending infantry reinforcements from Egypt by way of the Black Sea. Unfortunately for the Poles, the French assurances were largely a diplomatic maneuver to persuade the Soviet Union to join an anti-German front. The French had no intention of keeping their part of the bargain. For one thing, the French intelligence service had grossly overestimated the strength of Germany's West Wall. Remembering the devastation France suffered during the Great War, the high command was not about to mount a major offensive into Germany without meticulous preparation; fifteen days was simply not enough time.

Most of Poland's fighter planes were obsolescent PZL-P.11s such as these. With a top speed of 243 miles per hour, the gull-wing PZL-P.11 was no match for the much-faster Messerschmitts.

Buoyed by the pledges of their allies—however vague or false—and convinced that the Soviets would remain neutral, the Polish generals were optimistic that they could fight the Germans. They envisioned a rerun of the 1920 Polish-Soviet war: Their tough, well-trained infantry would draw the enemy either toward fixed fortifications behind the border or deep into Polish territory, until the magnificent Polish horse cavalry could slash into the Germans' rear, severing their lines of supply and communication. Poland was well prepared for such a campaign. Indeed, the army, when fully mobilized, numbered more than 1.75 million troops, and another 500,000 were in reserve.

Behind this strength in personnel, however, lurked appalling weaknesses. Polish military doctrine placed small value on staff officers. As a result, fewer than one in twenty army leaders had received specialized training. For communications, the army relied on the inadequate civil telephone and telegraph network. Poland's 800 tanks were obsolete French models or Polish-built vehicles patterned on British prototypes. Instead of being grouped together, they were parceled out among the infantry units. The Polish field artillery was armed with a copy of the excellent French 77-mm

Polish cavalry advances at a trot during prewar maneuvers. While European armies were phasing out the horse cavalry, Poland kept forty mounted regiments. They were needed because of a shortage of motor vehicles, poor roads, and the cavalry's ability to function during the rainy season, when much of the countryside became a marsh.

gun, but the heavy artillery was woefully out-of-date. Modern 105- and 155-mm howitzers had been slow in reaching operational units. The gunners' fire-control equipment was obsolete, and to confound matters, few artillery regiments had their full complement of transportation. In the early 1930s, the Polish air force's fighter planes had been among the best in the world, but now they were obsolescent. All too many of the 935 planes were suitable only for training.

The Polish defensive plan also was defective. The generals expected the Germans to try to cut the corridor while a second force advanced from Silesia toward Warsaw. The Poles planned to meet every German attack near the border, using their as-yet-incomplete fortifications to cover possible lines of advance. At worst, they would conduct a fighting retreat eastward, bleeding the enemy until pressure from France and Britain compelled the German command to withdraw some forces to face the threat in the west. Then the cavalry would strike.

Accordingly, the Poles placed seven armies in the paths of the expected invasion. Counterclockwise from the north, they included the Narew Group and the Modlin Army, south of the East Prussian border; the Pomorze Army, in the lower corridor; the Poznan Army, in Poland's westernmost bulge into Germany; the Lodz Army, midway between Warsaw and the closest approach of the German border; the Krakow Army, in the southwest, facing the junction of the German and Slovak borders; and the little Carpathian Army of mountain troops, behind the rugged peaks that demarcated the southern border of Poland. A general reserve was to be held to the south of the capital, but the eastern border with the Soviet Union would be left unprotected.

The scheme did not impress the French chief of staff, General Maurice Gamelin, who tried to persuade the Poles to concentrate a line of defense through the nation's midsection, roughly along the Vistula River in front of Warsaw. But this strategy was politically unacceptable to Polish leaders. The country's will to resist, it was thought, could not survive ceding the densely populated agricultural and industrial areas of the west to the Germans in the first hours of engagement.

What neither the Polish generals nor anyone else outside Germany expected was that the onslaught would be one the world had never seen before. Although most members of the German high command expected to win with their superb infantry, artillery, and air power, the Wehrmacht had received approval to test these branches, combined with the new panzer divisions of armor and motorized infantry, in a tactical concept called blitzkrieg, or lightning war. The idea of overwhelming the enemy with one quick punch of blinding speed and tremendous force appealed to Hitler. More critical, he knew that Germany lacked the industrial capacity and the psychological readiness for protracted fighting. And he was determined not to repeat the debilitating trench warfare of 1914-1918.

While the generals prepared, the diplomats came to a tense stalemate in the late summer of 1939. Then an announcement from Berlin burst like a bombshell over the European landscape. At eleven o'clock on Monday evening, August 21, a bulletin interrupted a musical program on German radio; Germany and Russia had concluded a nonaggression pact.

It was an astonishing alliance between two regimes that until now had seemed to be archenemies. While the British and French had been negotiating fruitlessly with the evasive Soviets, Russian and German diplomats had been holding secret parleys. Ostensibly, they had been talking about trade, but in reality they had pursued a larger agenda that became public only with the announcement of the final agreement. Despite their glaring ideological differences, the two totalitarian powers had one view in common: They despised the Western democracies. Stalin, for his part, believed he could postpone, or eliminate, a conflict between the Soviet Union and Germany by turning the Nazis against the West until Russia was strong enough to face Germany or the tensions between them evaporated. Hitler believed he had sidestepped the possibility of a two-front war against major powers—at least for now. Suddenly, Poland was presented with an enemy on its eastern frontier for which it had not prepared. Moreover, a secret protocol to the nonaggression pact envisioned Russian annexation of half of Poland as well as Latvia and Estonia.

On August 22, the day before Ribbentrop flew to Moscow to sign the agreement, Hitler called in his senior military commanders and instructed them to invade Poland at a quarter past four in the morning on August 26. Perhaps the British and French would back down, perhaps not; his only fear now, he told the assembled officers, was that "at the last minute some *Schweinhund* will make a proposal for mediation."

The next day, Chamberlain warned Hitler: If Germany invaded Poland, the British would attack Germany with "all the forces at their command, and it is impossible to foresee the end of hostilities, once engaged." Now there could be no doubt; an attack on Poland would mean war. Mussolini, however, declined Hitler's request for help against Poland because Italy was not ready for an all-out conflict. At least briefly, Hitler blinked. He postponed the invasion.

The Führer tried the familiar tactic of raging at the British ambassador, Henderson, but to no avail. Then he made the preposterous offer that if Great Britain and France stood aside while Germany took Poland, he would guarantee the continued existence of the British empire and respect the existing borders of France. While rejecting this outlandish proposal, the British and French continued to cast about for a way to avoid the inevitable, importuning against the full mobilization of the Polish army for fear the move would anger Hitler. The Poles concurred, hesitant to appear the aggressor and feeling that mobilization might block a last-minute settlement. In round-the-clock maneuvers, the British pleaded for three-way negotiations. The Germans demanded that the Poles immediately send to Berlin a representative possessing full authority to act on behalf of the Polish government. The British negotiators, realizing that this would be tantamount to a Polish surrender, refused to pass the demand on to the Poles until after its expiration.

The German people knew little about these feverish diplomatic exchanges. Their newspapers and radios told them that Poland was in chaos, that Polish troops were persecuting German expatriates and threatening Germany's borders. Poland had been unpopular in Germany since its seizure of Silesia in 1919, and the prospect of punishing the upstart next-door was satisfying. But on Monday, August 28, Germans were suddenly confronted with food-rationing cards, issued prematurely when Hitler's order postponing the attack on Poland was not conveyed to the Agriculture Ministry. The cards were an unsettling reminder of hardships endured during the Great War, after a local conflict became global.

"The average German today looks dejected," the American correspondent William L. Shirer wrote from Berlin on August 29. "He can't get over the blow of the ration cards, which to him spells war. On a night when everyone

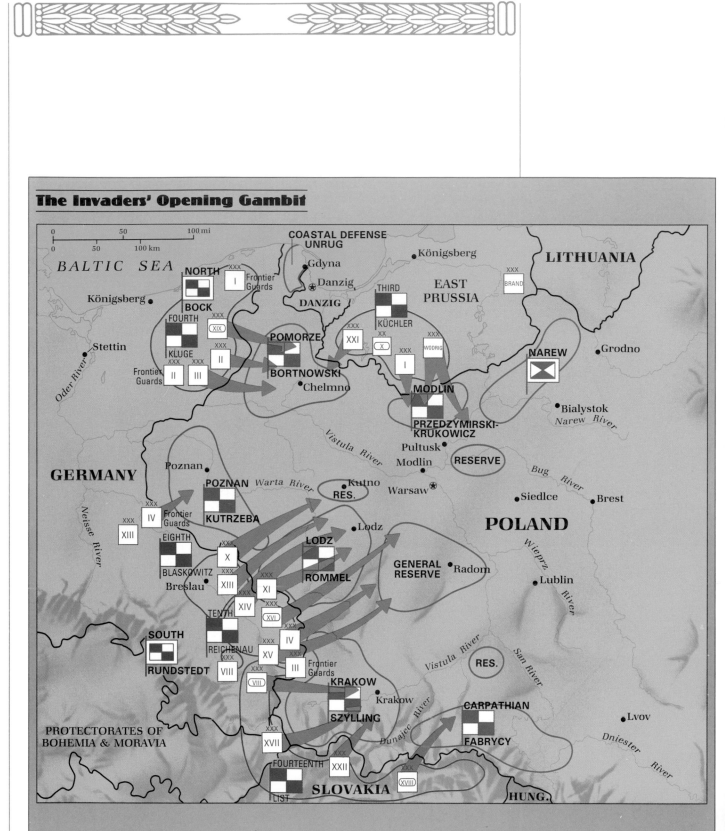

The Invaders' Opening Gambit

The plan for the invasion of Poland called for a massive pincer movement that would snap shut around Warsaw, the capital, crushing Polish forces in a steel vice. Arrows trace the moves by Army Group North and Army Group South during the first six days of the German campaign. In the north, the Fourth Army sliced across the Polish Corridor, sealing off Danzig, and the Third Army drove southward from East Prussia. In the south, the attacking Eighth and the Tenth armies rolled toward Warsaw as the Fourteenth Army advanced on the city of Krakow.

knew the issue of war or peace might be decided, less than 500 people out of a population of five million turned out in front of the chancellery. These few stood there grim and silent."

Hitler had decided on war. In order to inflame public opinion at home and assuage it in the rest of the world, he arranged a ghastly skit. Late on August 31, with the German armies already in motion, an SS squad in civilian clothes ordered a dozen concentration-camp inmates to put on Polish army uniforms. All but one of the prisoners were marched into a woods ten miles from the Polish border and executed. The SS men then hustled the surviving inmate to a nearby radio station. They burst in, seized a microphone, broadcast an announcement in Polish that Poland was invading Germany, shot the remaining prisoner, and left. The evidence was clear, Hitler would proclaim over and over again: Germany had been invaded and was only protecting itself.

At half past six in the evening on August 31, Lipski paid one last call on Ribbentrop. Before entering the foreign minister's office, the Polish diplomat paused to cast a lingering glance at the table at which he had signed the nonaggression treaty five years earlier. Then he went in, only to be ejected because he lacked full plenipotentiary powers. The German government then concocted a story blaming the Poles for refusing to send a representative to discuss a list of sixteen German proposals.

The Second World War began in Danzig, a half-hour ahead of schedule. At 4:17 a.m. on Friday, September 1, a group of overzealous Nazi irregulars surrounded the Polish post office and demanded its surrender. The response was a hail of gunfire—the postal workers in that troubled city were armed—and a small but bitter engagement began that would last all day.

Citizens awakened by the small-arms fire thought they were hearing another skirmish in the long agony of the free city, but the booming sounds from the harbor at a quarter of five could not be dismissed so lightly. The obsolete but still potent German battleship *Schleswig-Holstein*, supposedly on a ceremonial visit, opened fire at point-blank range on the Westerplatte, an old fortress located four miles north of Danzig where the Poles had a military installation. About the same time, other sounds of doomsday reverberated over Poland as the German air force dropped bombs on air bases, railroads, highways, and cities.

The air attacks were not the overwhelming successes that Luftwaffe planners had envisioned. Thick fog over northern Poland aborted a massive raid on Warsaw and hampered the ability of the pilots to find their targets. In the south, where the weather was better, the Germans had hoped to catch the Polish planes on the ground, but the Poles had already dispersed

With a salvo heard around the world, the German battleship *Schleswig-Holstein* opens fire at close range against the Polish munitions depot at the Westerplatte, near Danzig, in the predawn hours of September 1, 1939. At left, SS troops move through Danzig later in the day, mopping up Polish resistance.

most of their fighters to auxiliary airstrips, and those that remained courageously took to the sky. The Polish pilots exacted a price from the German bombers but could barely slow the onslaught. The bombers, escorted by Messerschmitt 110 fighters, shattered the country's rail system, which was clogged with nearly a million soldiers responding to mobilization orders issued the previous day.

All along the 1,750-mile border between Poland and Germany's possessions, the chatter of German machine guns erupted and engines roared as the massed tanks of the panzer divisions rumbled toward their assigned targets. Grinning infantrymen stopped to smash barriers and pull down border signs for the benefit of the propaganda corps's photographers. From East Prussia, the German Third Army, commanded by Lieutenant General Georg von Küchler, launched two assaults, sending its I Corps and Corps Wodrig hurtling southward toward Warsaw and the XXI Corps southwestward into the base of the corridor. Lieutenant General Günther von Kluge's Fourth Army, whose XIX Corps was led by Lieutenant General Heinz Guderian, the army's foremost proponent of mechanized warfare, drove east into the corridor from Pomerania.

Ground operations in the north, like the air attacks, were hampered by

The Ju 87B-1 carried either a 1,102-pound bomb as shown here, or a 550-pound bomb with four additional 110-pounders attached to the wings. A boom was used to sling bombs mounted under the fuselage around the propeller in order to avoid damage during a dive.

Stuka: Agent of Terror

The flights of the ungainly, gull-wing Junkers 87s that led the way into Poland on September 1, 1939, added a dread new word to the lexicon of war: *Stuka*, short for *Sturzkampfflugzeug*, or dive bomber. Stukas spearheaded the blitzkrieg, destroying objectives with pinpoint accuracy or supporting the ground forces as airborne artillery.

The Ju 87's stable flight characteristics and robust construction made it popular with aircrews. The average pilot could deliver a bombload within thirty yards of the target, and the whine of the airstream over the plane's less-than-sleek fuselage, enhanced by wind-driven dive sirens, terrorized its victims even before the bombs fell.

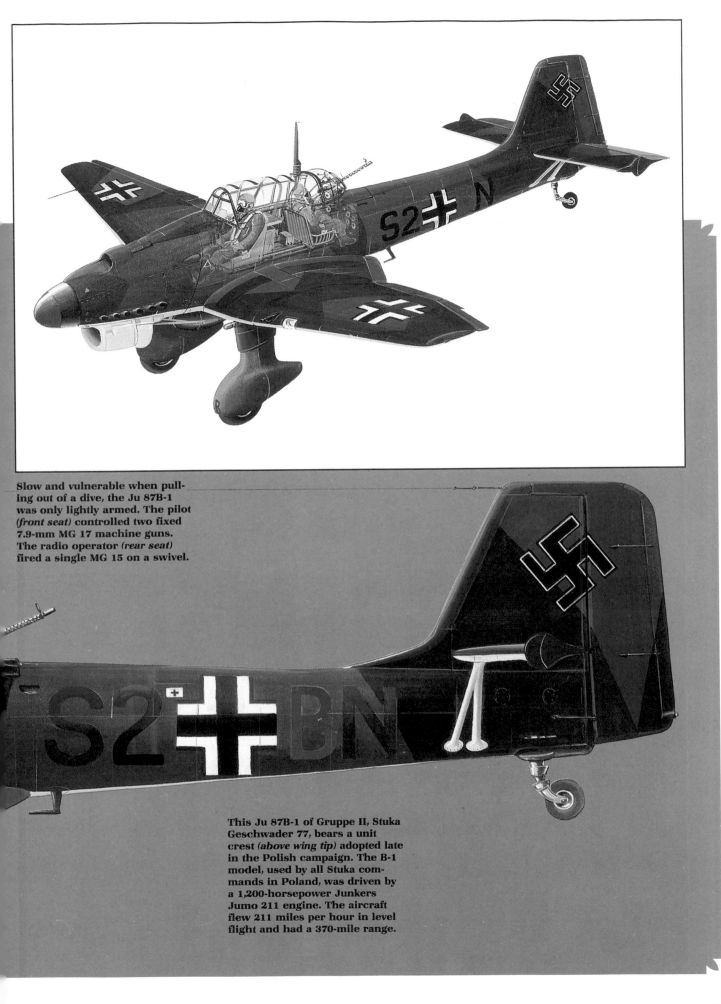

Slow and vulnerable when pulling out of a dive, the Ju 87B-1 was only lightly armed. The pilot *(front seat)* controlled two fixed 7.9-mm MG 17 machine guns. The radio operator *(rear seat)* fired a single MG 15 on a swivel.

This Ju 87B-1 of Gruppe II, Stuka Geschwader 77, bears a unit crest *(above wing tip)* adopted late in the Polish campaign. The B-1 model, used by all Stuka commands in Poland, was driven by a 1,200-horsepower Junkers Jumo 211 engine. The aircraft flew 211 miles per hour in level flight and had a 370-mile range.

murky weather. Air and artillery support of the infantry was of no use, adding to the confusion of troops coming under fire for the first time. Guderian was in the only place an armored-corps commander could function, an armored vehicle with the lead elements of his panzer division. He recalled that as German artillerists fired into the fog, "despite having received precise orders not to do so," they neatly bracketed his command vehicle with a shell in front and a shell behind. Reckoning that the third round would be a direct hit, Guderian ordered his driver to take evasive action. Unnerved, the man drove into a ditch at full speed, wrecking the vehicle but miraculously leaving Germany's top tank expert unhurt.

The fog soon lifted, and German forces rolled into the Polish Corridor with increasing speed. The I Frontier Guard Corps severed the corridor at its northern end, and Brigade Eberhard, a mixed force comprising SS and local militia, took Danzig—except for the Westerplatte garrison north of the city. At Gdynia, a Polish port that lies ten miles north of Danzig, the Germans ran into stiff opposition. Meanwhile, the Fourth Army headed across the corridor at its wider base in order to cut the Polish line of retreat and link up with the Third Army.

Third Army tanks of Panzer Division Kempf, fighting their way south across the corridor toward Warsaw, came up against some of Poland's strongest fortifications—concrete emplacements equipped with antitank guns—at Mlawa, just over the East Prussian border. Instead of following Guderian's doctrine and bypassing the city for later attention, they tried to punch their way through and were halted with heavy losses.

In the south, the main German assault was entrusted to the Tenth Army, which headed northeastward toward Warsaw. The Eighth Army, on its left, headed toward Lodz. The Fourteenth, on its right, followed the Vistula toward Krakow. Here, in clear weather, with air reconnaissance unhindered, the blitzkrieg tactics were executed with textbook precision. The armor simply bypassed enemy strongpoints and continued on its way. Then the Stukas, or dive bombers, came screeching out of the sky to pummel the defenders, who scarcely had time to catch their breath before being enveloped by the infantry. In many cases, the German air support routed the Polish rear guards before the panzers even arrived. By afternoon, elements of the Tenth Army were fifteen miles inside Poland. Behind them, the Frontier Guards and police units assumed control of the rear areas.

On the morning of the second day, the Fourth Army's leading panzer unit, Guderian's XIX Corps, ran out of gasoline and ammunition. But before the retreating Poles could realize their advantage, German supply columns fought their way through the confusion and got the tanks moving again. A short time later, the Fourth Army sealed the base of the corridor, trapping

Carrying its first trophy of war—a border marker bearing the Polish eagle—a German staff car leads a column of vehicles into Poland. Although Nazi propaganda depicted the Wehrmacht as highly motorized, most of the infantry advanced on foot.

within it two infantry divisions of the Pomorze Army and the Pomorska Cavalry Brigade. The encircled cavalry attempted and failed to break out, a heroic effort that spawned the enduring legend of Polish lancers galloping suicidally toward Nazi tanks.

On the stalled Third Army's front at Mlawa, units from Corps Wodrig finally broke through the ring of fortresses east of the city while Panzer Division Kempf redeployed, successfully outflanking the Mlawa defenses on the south. By September 3, the Polish Modlin Army was in full retreat, leaving behind more than 10,000 prisoners of war.

The swiftly changing battlefield called for new German tactics. The commander of Army Group North, General Fedor von Bock, consulted hastily with Field Marshal Walther von Brauchitsch of the army high command. Despite his concern that the armored forces might advance too far to face a sudden emergency on Germany's western borders, Brauchitsch permitted Bock to send the Fourth Army's XIX Corps on a sweep deep into eastern Poland.

The remnants of the Pomorze Army fled to the southwest, toward Warsaw, leaving behind 15,000 prisoners and ninety artillery pieces. By this time, the Modlin Army was also falling back on the capital, and the Narew Group was withdrawing eastward toward Bialystok. Only the trapped defenders of Gdynia and the Hel Peninsula at the northern tip of the corridor continued to fight.

Meanwhile, Germany's massive Army Group South, commanded by General Gerd von Rundstedt, lumbered across the Polish plain toward Warsaw from the southwest at a pace of better than ten miles a day. The Fourteenth Army's main body advanced on Krakow while its XXII Corps, augmented by Slovak troops, fought its way through passes guarded by crack Polish mountain regiments to flank the city from the south. In the center, tanks from the 4th Panzer Division of Lieutenant General Walther von Reichenau's Tenth Army bulled through modest Polish resistance. To their north, the two infantry corps of Lieutenant General Johannes Blaskowitz's Eighth Army pushed toward Lodz. On and on the Germans pressed, through the panic and confusion ignited by their appearance, giving the Poles no time to comprehend what was happening. When the Poles blew up a bridge, German engineers swiftly threw pontoons across the water. When the Poles tried to regroup, Stukas broke up their formations before they could counterattack. The Polish high command in Warsaw, which had unwisely set out to control each of its seven armies without an intervening level of command, was now completely out of touch with its soldiers in the field.

In desperation, the Polish government appealed to Britain and France. The British cabinet had met late in the morning of September 1 but declared the situation too confusing to merit action, despite receiving word from the British ambassador in Warsaw that he could hear bombs falling. After worried consultations, the British and French contented themselves with issuing a warning to Germany.

On the second day of the invasion, while Beck and his ambassadors pleaded for their allies to fulfill their obligations, the British and French waited for an answer from Germany. It never came. Not until Prime Minister Chamberlain faced a revolt by the House of Commons did he agree to present the Germans with an ultimatum. With the last hope for peace gone, a despairing Chamberlain admitted, "Everything I have worked for, everything I have hoped for, everything I have believed in, has crashed in ruins."

Reluctantly, the French followed suit. These last preliminaries to war were delivered on Sunday, September 3. The British warning expired at 11 a.m., the French at 5 p.m. As of that time, both Britain and France were officially at war with Germany. Still they took no action.

By September 5, the German Tenth Army was halfway to Warsaw, sixty miles inside Poland and sixty miles from the capital. Its 2d and 3d Light Divisions were fighting outside Radom, preparing to cross the Vistula to encircle Warsaw from the southeast. The Eighth Army, on the Tenth's left, was approaching Lodz; the Fourteenth, on the right, was about to take Krakow. An exuberant Hitler toured the battlefield in the north and found it difficult to believe how effective the blitzkrieg had been. General Guderian showed the Führer the remains of a Polish artillery regiment that, like many

A Harsh Introduction to Combat

Officers and enlisted men of the Leibstandarte SS Adolf Hitler take a break on a dusty Polish road as a building burns behind them.

An anonymous combat photographer vividly recorded one German regiment's trial by fire during the conquest of Poland. The pictures are reproduced above and on the pages that follow. The Leibstandarte SS Adolf Hitler, a motorized infantry regiment that until recently had served as the Führer's bodyguard, was yanked from combat training and sent into action at the forefront of the Eighth Army's thrust toward Warsaw. Although the regiment would earn high marks for courage, the green troops suffered from inexperience and do-or-die recklessness.

Led by General Josef "Sepp" Dietrich, the Leibstandarte seized key border crossings on September 1. But as the regiment moved deeper into Poland, it bogged down repeatedly in vicious street-fighting. At the town of Pabianice, Polish troops surrounded Dietrich's men, who had to be rescued by a regiment of the regular army. As the Leibstandarte neared Warsaw on September 9, it suffered heavy casualties while fending off Polish forces that were trying to break through the Eighth Army's lines and join their comrades defending the capital.

In time, the Polish defenses gave way, and the German army prevailed. The Leibstandarte, however, paid a stiff price in its first campaign: More than 400 of its members were killed or wounded.

Tanks of the 4th Panzers, which included the Leibstandarte, ford a stream west of Warsaw to intercept a retreating Polish column.

Rifles at the ready, SS men herd Polish families from their village. The wary Germans believed that civilians shot at passing units.

Leibstandarte troops rest beside a road, waiting for German artillery to blast through the defenses of Pabianice *(background)*.

Their rifles stacked, Leibstandarte soldiers examine a Polish armored train that was destroyed by the regiment's antitank guns.

Polish bodies line a ditch by the "road of death" at Oltarzew, where the Germans wiped out a large defending force on September 10.

others, had been caught completely off guard by the appearance of tanks far behind the supposed front. Hitler did not comprehend the meaning of the destruction. "Our dive bombers did that?" he asked. Guderian was pleased to set him right. "No," he replied proudly, "our panzers."

Guderian was also pleased to report that in his four divisions, totaling about 48,000 troops, there had been only 850 casualties thus far. Hitler recalled that on the first day of World War I, his regiment alone had lost 2,000 men. Guderian pressed home the point. "Tanks," the commander said, "are a lifesaving weapon."

Late in the afternoon on September 8, the leading elements of the Eighth Army's 4th Panzer Division, under Major General Georg-Hans Reinhardt, reached the perimeter of Warsaw. But their advance revealed that Warsaw was strongly fortified. The panzers, attacking the next morning without antitank support, were stopped cold by massed Polish field artillery and a handful of 7TP tanks. The following day, September 10, as they pulled back to await the arrival of heavy artillery and infantry, the German invasion encountered its first real trouble.

In its drive on Lodz, General Blaskowitz's Eighth Army, strengthened by the XI and XVI Corps from the Tenth Army, had bypassed an entire Polish army. The Polish force included four infantry divisions and two cavalry brigades, which had been positioned in the western bulge of Poland around the city of Poznan. The German command had assumed that the Poles were retreating eastward in order to escape double envelopment by the forces flanking it to the north and south. The Germans were confident that when they closed their pincers at Warsaw they could turn on the Poznan forces and annihilate them.

The Poles, however, did not follow the German scenario. Instead of retreating, the Poznan Army gathered the remnants of the shattered Pomorze Army from the Polish Corridor and reorganized. Most of the German air spotters who might have reported this peril were flying in front of their advancing divisions. To make matters worse, the spotters were having trouble sorting out what they were seeing on the ground below; the dense dust clouds raised by the movement of people and vehicles on the dry roads—Poland's annual rainy season had not yet begun—made it difficult to distinguish friend from foe.

At noon on September 10, the Poznan Army struck southward from the vicinity of Kutno, seventy miles west of Warsaw, into the exposed left flank of the German Eighth Army. When the blow came, the 30th Infantry Division, detailed to guard the flank, was marching hard to get into position. Its foot soldiers and horse-drawn supply wagons were stretched over twenty miles. The Polish attack seriously threatened Army Group South's plans. If the Poles severed the German line of advance, the Tenth Army would have to turn around to confront the danger. The Poles would have time to consolidate their defense of Warsaw and the Vistula, making the conquest of the eastern half of the country far more costly.

For two days, the Poles bludgeoned their way into the extended lines of the Eighth Army while the Germans struggled to organize a defense. Blaskowitz diverted his X Corps northward to assist the beleaguered 30th Division, and by September 11 a new German line was established. Engineer and antitank units from the Eighth Army rushed in to stiffen the line.

General Rundstedt, commanding Army Group South, refused to relinquish his position in front of the Polish capital; instead, he sought to turn the Poznan Army's attack to his advantage. He ordered Lieutenant General Ritter von Leeb to send his two XI Corps divisions slashing northward toward Kutno to sever the Pomorze Army from Warsaw and drive it west to the Bzura River, thus encircling it, along with the survivors of General Josef Rommel's Lodz Army. Meanwhile, the Eighth Army shifted northeastward into the fighting. At the same time, the Fourth Army moved south in order to close an iron ring around the embattled Poles in what came to be known as the Kutno Pocket.

By September 12, the Polish counterattack was spent, and the Poznan Army changed course. Its goal now was to escape entrapment and reach Warsaw, where it could help defend the capital. But the speed of the German mechanized divisions proved decisive, and the Poles could not break free. Division after division wore itself out against the Tenth Army, interposed between them and Warsaw. As the encircling Germans herded the Poles closer together, the Luftwaffe pounded them with increasing effectiveness. On September 17, after the Tenth Army had completed the destruction of the Polish forces around Radom, the Poznan Army collapsed. The Germans took 52,000 prisoners. The last functioning field army defending Poland, containing more than one-third of its effective ground forces, had been destroyed.

The German pincers, consisting of the Third and Fourth armies from the north and the Eighth and Tenth from the south, joined forces in front of Warsaw. In addition, they had improvised a second, outer set of pincers to envelop the fleeing armies from the rear. Guderian's corps from the north and elements of the Fourteenth Army from the south were arcing toward each other far to the east of the Vistula. On September 9, Major General Ferdinand Schaal's 10th Panzer Division had reinforced Guderian's XIX Corps. Guderian drove southward toward Brest, east of the Bug River. His panzers and motorized infantry rapidly left their flanking infantry behind

Closing a Double Pincers

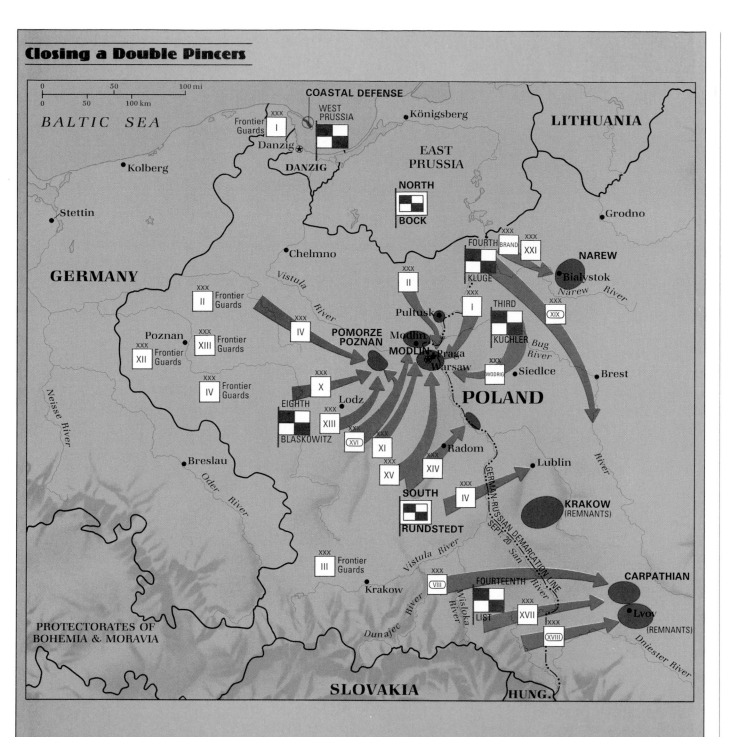

After three weeks of blitzkrieg, General Bock's Army Group North and General Rundstedt's Army Group South had penetrated deep into Poland *(red arrows)*, encircling or driving before them the Polish armies *(blue circles)*. As the German pincers closed around the remnants of the Pomorze and Poznan armies at Kutno and pushed units of the Lodz and Modlin armies back toward Warsaw, the Third Army's I Corps invested the capital from the east, cutting off possible retreat. To the south, elements of the German Tenth Army surrounded units of the Lodz Army at Radom while the Fourteenth Army drove the Krakow and the Carpathian armies eastward toward Lublin. Now the left wing of Army Group North and the right wing of Army Group South launched an even wider envelopment—a second pincer movement extending eastward to the Nazi-Soviet demarcation line. In the north, XIX Corps of the Fourth Army raced 100 miles east of Warsaw to Bialystok, where units of the Narew Group were regrouping, and to Brest, on the Bug River. In the south, XXII and XVII Corps of the Fourteenth Army attacked Lvov. By September 17, when the two arms of the outer pincers met, all that remained for the German conquerors was to capture isolated Warsaw and snuff out scattered pockets of Polish resistance at Kock in the southeast and on the Hel Peninsula near Danzig in the north.

A Polish heath is strewn with the carnage of horse-drawn artillery caught in the open by Stukas. The column had fought as part of the Pomorze Army, assigned to defend the Polish Corridor.

when Polish fortifications at Nowogrod held up the infantrymen. Three days before the Poznan Army disintegrated, Guderian's panzers had captured Brest, more than 100 miles due east of the capital. Warsaw was obviously doomed. So sudden was the XIX Corps's advance that at Zhabinka, near Brest, a Polish tank unit had been destroyed while it was still unloading from its railway cars.

Poland's only hope was to order every surviving unit to move south and west of the capital, into a tongue of Polish territory that protruded between Rumania and Hungary. There, with their backs to friendly territory, the remnants of the Polish army would try to hold out until the Western allies came to their aid. But by September 17, it was apparent that a gap yawned between French and British promises and their performance. France had perfunctorily fulfilled its obligation to conduct a diversionary attack by sending nine divisions seven miles into German territory, across the Saar River to the vicinity of the West Wall. It was hardly necessary for the Germans to alert their forces facing the French, let alone pull any divisions from Poland. Instead of launching an all-out attack, the French commander sent the Poles a message of sympathy: "With all my heart, I share your anguish and have faith in the tenacity of your resistance."

The British bombing also smacked of timidity. Following a policy intended to avoid excessive civilian casualties, the Royal Air Force was content to drop a few bombs on isolated military targets and rain propaganda leaflets over the Rhineland—the source of most of the ordnance being expended against the Poles.

As disheartened as the Poles might have been by their allies' fecklessness, these worries paled into insignificance in the face of a separate development on September 17. It began at three in the morning with a summons to the Polish ambassador in Moscow; he was to appear at once at the Soviet Foreign Ministry. When the envoy arrived, he was shocked to hear the deputy Soviet foreign minister proclaim, "The Polish government has disintegrated and no longer shows any sign of life." The official expressed concern for the welfare of the "kindred Ukrainian and White Russian people who live on Polish territory." The Soviet Union intended to protect these people, he said, and furthermore to "extricate the Polish people from the unfortunate war into which they were dragged by their unwise leaders." As the Polish ambassador tried to comprehend this news, the Red Army, thirty-five divisions strong, was already pouring across the 800-mile-long border between Russia and Poland.

Stalin had delayed as long as he could. Mobilizing the Red Army was a slow and cumbersome process, and Soviet propaganda had yet to explain why the leader of worldwide communism had entered into a treaty with the hated fascists. Now Stalin realized he must act. Some German units were already east of the line (from East Prussia to Warsaw along the Narew River, then southward to Slovakia along the Vistula and Bug rivers) along which he and Hitler had agreed to partition Poland.

The German high command had not been told of the impending Soviet move until days before the Red Army invaded Poland, and the news filtered through the chain of command slowly. When the units conducting the outer pincer movement received orders to withdraw, their commanders were mystified. Many were heavily engaged with Polish forces and had thousands of wounded to care for, prisoners to guard, and vehicles to repair. With great difficulty they disentangled themselves and pulled back to the demarcation line.

The situation of the remaining Polish forces, most of which were concentrating at the so-called Rumanian Bridgehead in the far southeast, was

General Wladyslaw Bortnowski (right), commander of the Pomorze Army, and General Tadeusz Malinowski, deputy chief of staff, discuss Poland's plight. A few days later, Bortnowski was taken prisoner by the Germans. Malinowski escaped to France.

hopeless. The army was not ready to give up, but its leaders were. The government fled to the country of Rumania, following the commander in chief of the armed forces, Marshal Rydz-Smigly, who on the night of September 17 had left Poland without notifying either his government or his military subordinates.

Meanwhile, the German Third and Tenth armies besieging Warsaw were encountering spirited resistance and making slow headway. Hitler, after visiting the outskirts of the capital on September 22, ordered the Eighth Army to attack from the west. He wanted as much of the civilian population as possible driven eastward, into the section to be occupied by the Russians, so that the Germans would not be responsible for caring for them.

On the same day, General Werner von Fritsch was killed in action. A year earlier, Hitler had appointed him commander of the 12th Artillery Regiment—a sop to the disgraced general's constant requests for public exoneration. Fritsch's regiment formed the artillery element of the Third Army's 12th Division. As the division probed the area near Praga, Fritsch moved to the front lines to observe his unit in action. Refusing to take cover, he was struck down by a Polish bullet. His body was carried from the field in a common soldier's shelter half. Troops who saw him fall felt that Fritsch had sought his own death.

By September 26, the date of the major Eighth Army assault, the condition of Warsaw had become desperate. Food supplies were exhausted, and the water system was knocked out. The city contained 16,000 wounded

Below, German troops lie poised on the outskirts of Warsaw. Left, visiting a forward battery on September 24, Hitler watches the bombardment of the Polish capital through a telescope. "No soldier will die for prestige reasons," the Führer decreed. "The Luftwaffe and the artillery will destroy all essential installations. In three or four days, Warsaw will capitulate."

soldiers and many thousand more wounded civilians. The electric and telephone utilities no longer worked. After a day-long bombardment by artillery and the Luftwaffe, General Josef Rommel, commander of the forces defending Warsaw, requested a cease-fire to negotiate a surrender. The Germans refused, intensified the bombardment, and replied that only an unconditional surrender would be accepted. At midday on September 27, the Poles complied, and 140,000 troops surrendered. The 24,000-man garrison at nearby Modlin followed suit the next day.

The German forces were now free to concentrate against the remaining resistance at the Rumanian Bridgehead. Within a few days, they killed or

A turned-over streetcar provides a barricade for German infantrymen firing a machine gun during the investment of Warsaw. To worsen the city's food and water shortages and force a surrender, the soldiers followed instructions not to allow civilians to escape through their lines.

captured 150,000 Poles there. The rest, about 100,000, made their way to safety in Rumania—but only after fighting through the hostile Ukrainians who lived in the area.

While the steel jaws of the German pincers were snapping shut around Warsaw, two ragtag groups of Poles in the port area of the corridor, at Gdynia and on the Hel Peninsula, continued to resist. On September 19, the garrison at Gdynia gave up after shelling by the *Schleswig-Holstein* and bombing by Stukas destroyed its ammunition reserve. The Polish commander committed suicide rather than conduct the surrender.

Now the Germans focused on the 450 naval infantry and militiamen inside the Hel fortifications at the end of a seven-mile-long spit of land that jutted into the Baltic. The Poles, led by Rear Admiral Josef Unrug, had sown the narrow peninsula with mines. Coastal artillery covered the Poles' seaward side. On September 21, the garrison beat back a German land attack. Three days later, the *Schleswig-Holstein*, joined by its sister ship, the *Schlesien*, pounded the Poles unmercifully with their eleven-inch guns. The next day, Stukas destroyed the rail line the Poles used to move their big guns into firing position. On October 1, Unrug surrendered.

The fall of the Hel garrison left only a few pockets of resistance. The last organized Polish force—a 17,000-man garrison at Kock, seventy-five miles southeast of Warsaw—surrendered on October 6.

In thirty-six days, the German war machine had humbled a major European army. Twenty years after being dismantled by the Treaty of Versailles, it had inflicted more than 750,000 casualties while suffering a mere 8,082 killed, 5,029 missing, and 27,278 wounded. It had introduced a stunning new array of tactics that would transform modern warfare. But it had also encountered problems. Only one in six German divisions had been organized as panzer units, and these had not been consistently employed. Contrary to subsequent legend, a large portion of the army that invaded Poland had moved on foot and depended on horse-drawn supply wagons. The Germans, led by Hermann Göring, trumpeted their new Luftwaffe but avoided mention of the more than 400 planes that had been lost or severely damaged by an opponent with inferior aircraft.

No one was more impressed with the German showing than Hitler himself. In his estimation, success owed nothing to the technological shortcomings of the doughty Poles and everything to his resoluteness in overriding the caution of his military commanders. The same intuition that had told Hitler that Austria, Czechoslovakia, and Poland were ripe for plucking now urged him to unleash his forces on France and Britain, before they had time to gird for war. It was only with the utmost reluctance that he agreed with his generals to wait until spring. ✠

"The Enemy is at the Gates"

"The enemy is at the gates, and he sends his angels of death to proclaim his coming." So wrote Chaim Kaplan, a Warsaw school principal, as German bombers pounded the Polish capital in September 1939. "When the air-raid alarm is heard," said Kaplan, "the streets empty at once, and a terrible silence reigns. These are horrible moments. You are carried away on the wings of your sick imagination, as though the ceiling were falling on your head and you would not even be privileged to see those dearest to you before your death."

For the people of Warsaw, who wrestled with such fears day and night, the siege was an unmitigated ordeal. But for American photographer Julien Bryan, who had reached Warsaw by train from Rumania on September 7, shortly before the city was cut off, it represented the chance of a lifetime. The Polish government had fled two days earlier, and the American press corps had followed, abandoning the field to Bryan. As the Germans tightened their noose, however, Bryan wondered if he would survive the drama he was documenting. "I had the siege of Warsaw all to myself," he wrote later, "but I wasn't too happy about it."

By night, Bryan huddled with some seventy others in the basement of the American embassy; by day, he scoured the city, taking the pictures shown here—chronicles of carnage, sorrow, and defiance. The decision of the Polish authorities to defend the city at all costs led to punishing German onslaughts aimed at civilians and soldiers alike. On September 13, the Jewish section of the city was firebombed, a fate that was soon visited on other areas. A few days later, Bryan reported, German guns peppered the city with shells timed to explode above the streets, spraying those below with hot steel. On Warsaw's outskirts, fighter planes swooped low to strafe refugees and foragers.

Bryan's harrowing stint came to an end on September 21, when he and the other remaining neutrals in Warsaw were evacuated. For the city's own, however, the terror lasted another six days, until the Polish garrison surrendered. By then, Chaim Kaplan wrote, most residents had no food and water and could only wait as helplessly "for Hitler's army as for the spring rains." The Führer's army marched in on September 30, offering relief. But not all those in need accepted. A young woman who had lost her home to a bomb and a second place of refuge to fire, spurned the German troops: "I couldn't look at them. I felt such hatred." A few days later, she joined the underground resistance—a force that in the years to come would haunt Warsaw's occupiers like an avenging angel.

A volunteer policeman wearing an armband watches with two companions from the portico of the Warsaw Opera House as German warplanes approach. The column to his right, pitted by shell fragments, carries a poster urging Poles to arms. During the siege, the Luftwaffe employed a diverse arsenal, ranging from Stukas *(left)*, which zeroed in on their targets, to Ju 52 transports, which carpeted a broad area with incendiaries.

A soldier talks with his wife during the siege. Photographer Bryan noted that the defenders of the city contacted their kin out of fear for their safety: "Losses among civilians were greater than among soldiers, and often it was not so much a question of a husband returning alive from battle as of the family remaining alive at home."

Poles inspect the engine of a German bomber that was shot down over the capital. Watching from the roof of the American embassy, Bryan joined in the cheering as the plane crashed in flames, killing its crew of four. "We were glad they were dead. That is what war does to you."

Two Orthodox Jews build a barricade in Warsaw. Kaplan noted that many Jews turned out for such duty, mindful that "wherever Hitler's foot treads, there is no hope for the Jewish people."

Above, two Polish soldiers and a civilian plant a streetcar rail in order to complete an antitank barrier. At right, an overturned, bombed-out streetcar reinforces a line of obstacles constructed by the city's defenders. Such crude fortifications helped stymie a German panzer assault on Warsaw on September 8. The panzers then pulled back to await the arrival of the infantry and heavy artillery and additional raids by the Luftwaffe.

PRZYSTANEK
TRAMWAJÓW
MIEJSKICH

The crater above was gouged by one of five 500-pound bombs that fell with deadly effect on the buildings and grounds of a Warsaw hospital. The blasts tore away the end of a ward and littered debris on surgery patients.

Dead horses—a common sight during the siege—provided sustenance for the famished Poles. Even if the carcasses were rotting, Kaplan reported, people "would cut off chunks and eat them to quiet their hunger."

Women and children examine a Catholic church destroyed during mass on Sunday, September 10. Alerted by an air-raid alarm, the worshipers fled to safety before the bomb struck.

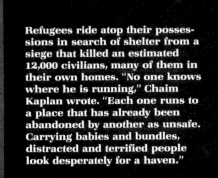

Refugees ride atop their possessions in search of shelter from a
siege that killed an estimated
12,000 civilians, many of them in
their own homes. "No one knows
where he is running," Chaim
Kaplan wrote. "Each one runs to
a place that has already been
abandoned by another as unsafe.
Carrying babies and bundles,
distracted and terrified people
look desperately for a haven."

Carrying on amid devastation, a boy chops kindling on a lot that is strewn with salvaged possessions as his aunt tends the kettle and a cousin washes her feet.

Outside the American embassy, a peasant sells milk fresh from a cow while her husband (*seated at right*) minds the animal and the family's bundled belongings.

Nurses tend to mothers and their babies in a damaged hospital. "Some women cried softly and others nursed their infants," Bryan noted, "as doctors bandaged babies who had been struck by shrapnel or broken glass."

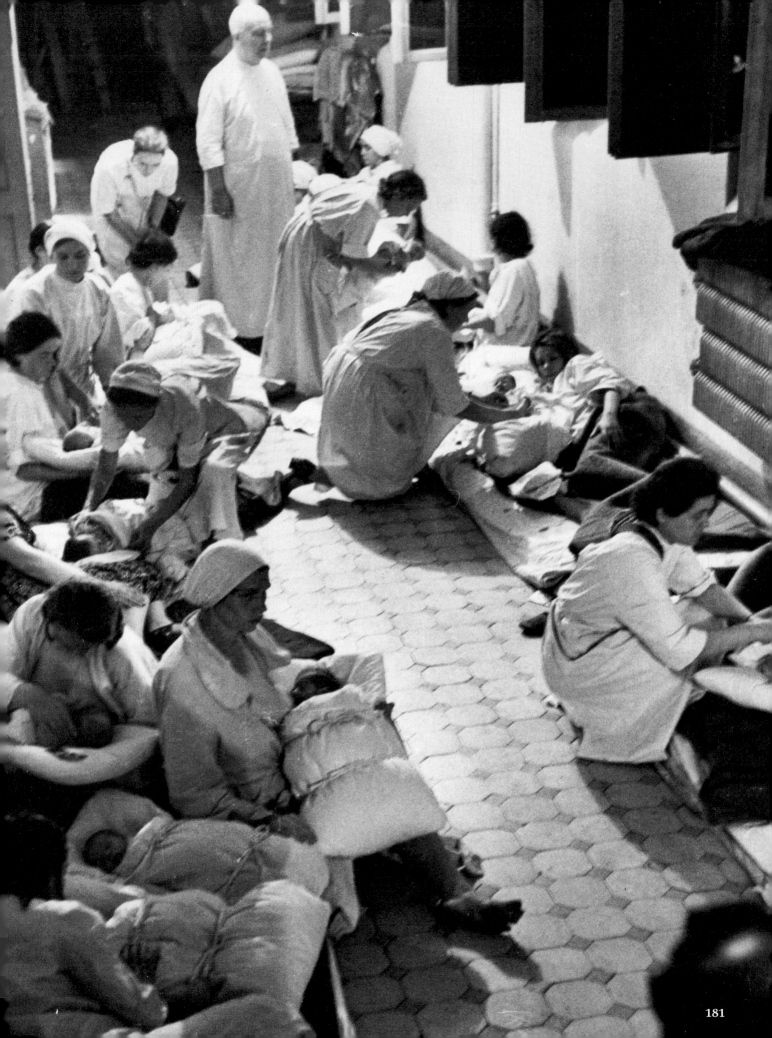

Above, a boy crouches fearfully
near the dead body of his
mother, one of several Warsaw
women who were digging
potatoes in a field when they
were strafed by German warplanes on September 14. At
right, a ten-year-old girl mourns
her sister, another victim of the
attack. Bryan recalled that the
youngster "leaned down and
touched the dead girl's face and
drew back in horror. 'O my
beautiful sister!' she wailed,
'What have they done to you?'"

Epitomizing the plight of civilians in a war that would grant them no quarter, nine-year-old Ryszard Pajewski sits dejectedly near a twisted bedstead and other remnants of a home destroyed. The siege, which claimed the life of Pajewski's younger brother, would be only the beginning of his family's ordeal: In 1940, the boy's father was taken to Germany as a slave laborer under a relocation plan that uprooted millions of Poles.

Acknowledgments

The editors thank the following individuals and institutions: England: Dorset—David Fletcher, Royal Armoured Corps Museum. London—Dr. Z. Jagodzinski, The Polish Library; Andrew Mollo; Alan Williams, Imperial War Museum; S. Zurakowski, The Polish Institute. South Croydon—Brian Leigh Davis. Federal Republic of Germany: Babenhausen—Heinz Nowarra. Berlin—Heidi Klein, Bildarchiv Preussischer Kulturbesitz; Gabrielle Kohler-Gallei,

Archiv für Kunst und Geschichte. Bonn —Holger Feldmann-Marth, Friedrich-Ebert-Stiftung. Bückeburg—Dr. Brigitte Porschmann, Niedersächsisches Staatsarchiv. Hamburg—Heinz Höhne. Hanover —Fritz Tobias. Koblenz—Meinrad Nilges, Bundesarchiv. Munich—Elisabeth Heidt, Süddeutscher Verlag Bilderdienst; Robert Hoffmann; Dr. Christian Zentner. Nuremberg—Günter Sengfelder. Stuttgart—Sabine Oppenländer, Institut für

Zeitgeschichte; Friedolf Schiek, Institut für Auslandsbeziehungen. France: Maisons-Alfort—Serge-Antoine Legrand. Paris—Christophe Thomas, Direction des Status et de l'Information, Ministère des Anciens Combattants. German Democratic Republic: Berlin—Hannes Quaschinsky, ADN-Zentralbild. United States: District of Columbia—Elizabeth Hill, National Archives; Eveline Nave, Library of Congress. Virginia—Krystyna Dunin-Borkowska.

Picture Credits

Credits from left to right are separated by semicolons, from top to bottom by dashes. Cover: CAF Photo Archives, Warsaw. 4-11: Hugo Jaeger, LIFE Magazine, © Time Inc. 12: AP/Wide World Photos. 14, 15: Map by R. R. Donnelley and Sons Company, Cartographic Services. 17: Bundesarchiv, Koblenz. 18: Ullstein Bilderdienst, West Berlin. 22, 23: Presseillustrationen Heinrich Hoffmann, Munich, except top right Keystone, Paris. 24, 25: Bundesarchiv, Koblenz. 26: Süddeutscher Verlag Bilderdienst, Munich. 28, 29: Ullstein Bilderdienst, West Berlin; UPI/Bettmann Newsphotos. 30: Süddeutscher Verlag Bilderdienst, Munich. 32, 33: AP/Wide World Photos. 35: Süddeutscher Verlag Bilderdienst, Munich. 36, 37: Hans Liska, *Signal*, May 1, 1940, Bundesarchiv Militärarchiv, Freiburg, courtesy Elisabeth Liska, Schesslitz; map by R. R. Donnelley and Sons Company, Cartographic Services—Library of Congress. 38-41: AP/Wide World Photos. 42: Süddeutscher Verlag Bilderdienst, Munich. 47: Lothar Rübelt, Vienna. 48, 49: Lothar Rübelt, Vienna, except top right Lothar Rübelt, from *Lothar Rübelt: Österreich zwischen den Kriegen,* © 1979 by Verlag Fritz Molden, Vienna. 50, 51: Lothar Rübelt, Vienna. 52, 53: Lothar Rübelt, Vienna; Library of Congress. 55: National Archives, no. 306-NT-969-43. 56: Bildarchiv Preussischer Kulturbesitz, West Berlin. 57, 58: Roger-Viollet, Paris. 60, 61: Library of

Congress, from *Der Freiheitskampf der Ostmark-Deutschen,* Leopold Stocker Verlag, Graz, 1942. 63: AP/Wide World Photos. 66: The Hulton Picture Company, London. 67: Ullstein Bilderdienst, West Berlin. 69: Archiv für Kunst und Geschichte, West Berlin. 70: UPI/Bettmann Newsphotos. 71: The Hulton Picture Company, London—Lothar Rübelt, Vienna. 73: AP/Wide World Photos. 74-81: Hugo Jaeger, LIFE Magazine, © Time Inc. 82: UPI/Bettmann Newsphotos. 84: Bildarchiv Preussischer Kulturbesitz, West Berlin. 85: Map by R. R. Donnelley and Sons Company, Cartographic Services. 86: Okrensi Archive, Cheb. 87: Courtesy Time Inc. Picture Collection. 88: Margaret Bourke-White for LIFE. 90, 91: John Phillips for LIFE; Margaret Bourke-White for LIFE. 92, 93: John Phillips for LIFE. 94: Popperfoto, London. 95: AP/Wide World Photos—John Phillips for LIFE. 97, 98: Keystone, Paris. 101: John Phillips for LIFE. 102: AP/Wide World Photos—Czechoslovak News Agency, Prague. 103, 104: Czechoslovak News Agency, Prague. 107: Archiv Gerstenberg, Wietze (2); Bundesarchiv, Koblenz. 108, 109: John Phillips for LIFE; Süddeutscher Verlag Bilderdienst, Munich. 110: The Hulton Picture Company, London. 111: Courtesy Time Inc. Picture Collection. 112, 113: Bundesarchiv, Koblenz; Czechoslovak News Agency, Prague. 114, 115: Ullstein Bilderdienst, West Berlin; the Polish Library, London.

116, 117: Library of Congress. 118, 119: The Polish Institute and Sikorski Museum, London; Library of Congress, from *Warszawa Stolica Polski,* Spoleczny Fundusz Odbudowy Stolicy, 1949 (2). 120, 121: Bildarchiv Preussischer Kulturbesitz, West Berlin; CAF Photo Archives, Warsaw. 122, 123: Roger-Viollet, Paris; Ullstein Bilderdienst, West Berlin. 124, 125: Courtesy George A. Petersen—art by Time-Life Books; Library of Congress. 126-134: Library of Congress. 137: AP/Wide World Photos. 140-143: Ullstein Bilderdienst, West Berlin. 144: Archives Tallandier, Paris. 145: A.F.P. (Paris). 148: Map by R. R. Donnelley and Sons Company, Cartographic Services. 150: Library of Congress, from *Danzig* by Carl Otto Windecker, copyright 1941 Schützen-Verlag, GmbH, Berlin SW 68. 151: Paramount News, courtesy Time Inc. Picture Collection. 152, 153: Art by John Batchelor. 155: Ullstein Bilderdienst, West Berlin. 157-160: Library of Congress. 163: Map by R. R. Donnelley and Sons Company, Cartographic Services. 164: Bildarchiv Preussischer Kulturbesitz, West Berlin. 165: UPI/Bettmann Newsphotos. 166: Library of Congress, from *Entscheidende Stunden* by Eric Borchert, Wilhelm Limpert-Verlag, Berlin SW 68, 1941. 167: Bildarchiv Preussischer Kulturbesitz, West Berlin. 168, 169: Library of Congress, from *Entscheidende Stunden* by Eric Borchert, Wilhelm Limpert-Verlag, Berlin SW 68, 1941. 170-185: Julien Bryan.

Bibliography

Books

Adamthwaite, Anthony, *France and the Coming of the Second World War, 1936-1939*. Totowa, N.J.: Frank Cass, 1977.

Addington, Larry H., *The Blitzkrieg Era and the German General Staff, 1865-1941*. New Brunswick, N.J.: Rutgers Univ. Press, 1972.

Bekker, Cajus, *The Luftwaffe War Diaries*. Ed. and transl. by Frank Ziegler. Garden City, N.Y.: Doubleday, 1968.

Berkley, George E., *Vienna and Its Jews*. Cambridge, Mass.: Abt Books, 1988.

Brook-Shepherd, Gordon:
   The Anschluss. Philadelphia: J. B. Lippincott, 1963.
   Dollfuss. London: Macmillan, 1961.

Brownell, Will, and Richard N. Billings, *So Close to Greatness*. New York: Macmillan, 1987.

Bryan, Julien, *Warsaw: 1939, Siege; 1959, Warsaw Revisited*. Warsaw, Poland: Polonia, 1960.

Bullock, Alan, *Hitler*. New York: Harper & Row, 1962.

Cecil, Robert, *The Myth of the Master Race*. New York: Dodd Mead, 1972.

Ciborowski, Adolf, *Warsaw: A City Destroyed and Rebuilt*. Warsaw, Poland: Polonia, 1965.

Cienciala, Anna M., *Poland and the Western Powers, 1938-1939*. London: Routledge & Kegan Paul, 1968.

Cooper, Matthew, *The German Army, 1933-1945*. London: Macdonald and Jane's, 1978.

Crankshaw, Edward, *Vienna*. London: Macmillan, 1976.

Deutsch, Harold C., *Hitler and His Generals: The Hidden Crisis, January-June 1938*. Minneapolis: Univ. of Minnesota Press, 1974.

Eubank, Keith, *Munich*. Westport, Conn.: Greenwood, 1984.

Fest, Joachim C., *Hitler*. Transl. by Richard Winston and Clara Winston. New York: Harcourt Brace Jovanovich, 1974.

François-Poncet, André, *The Fateful Years*. Transl. by Jacques LeClercq. New York: Harcourt, Brace, 1949.

Grasser, Kurt, and Jürgen Stahlmann, *Westwall, Maginot-Linie, Atlantikwall*. Leoni/Starnberger See, W.Ger.: Druffel-Verlag, 1983.

Green, William, *The Warplanes of the Third Reich*. Garden City, N.Y.: Doubleday, 1972.

Heineman, John L., *Hitler's First Foreign Minister*. Berkeley: Univ. of California Press, 1979.

Hillgruber, Andreas, *Germany and the Two World Wars*. Transl. by William C. Kirby. Cambridge, Mass.: Harvard Univ. Press, 1981.

Jagschitz, Gerhard, *Lothar Rübelt: Österreich zwischen den Kriegen*. Ed. by Christian Brandstätter. Vienna: Verlag Fritz Molden, 1979.

Kaplan, Chaim A., *Scroll of Agony*. Ed. and transl. by Abraham I. Katsh. New York: Macmillan, 1965.

Kennan, George F., *Memoirs, 1925-1950*. Boston: Little, Brown, 1972.

Kennedy, Paul, *The Rise and Fall of the Great Powers*. New York: Random House, 1987.

Kennedy, Robert M., "The German Campaign in Poland, 1939." Department of the Army Pamphlet No. 20-255. Washington: Department of the Army, 1956.

Lehmann, Rudolf, *The Leibstandarte*. Transl. by Nick Olcott. Winnipeg: J. J. Fedorowicz, 1987.

MacDonald, Charles B., *The Siegfried Line Campaign* (United States Army in World War II series). Washington: Office of the Chief of Military History, 1963.

Noakes, J., and G. Pridham, eds., *The Rise to Power, 1919-1934*. Vol. 1 of *Nazism, 1919-1945*. Exeter, England: Univ. of Exeter, 1983.

O'Neill, Robert J., *The German Army and the Nazi Party, 1933-1939*. New York: James H. Heineman, 1966.

Pauley, Bruce F., *Hitler and the Forgotten Nazis: A History of Austrian National Socialism*. Chapel Hill: Univ. of North Carolina Press, 1981.

Rich, Norman, *Hitler's War Aims*. New York: W. W. Norton, 1973.

Ries, Karl, Jr., *Markings and Camouflage Systems of Luftwaffe Aircraft in World War II*. Finthen, W.Ger.: Verlag Dieter Hoffmann, 1963.

Robertson, E. M., *Hitler's Pre-War Policy and Military Plans, 1933-1939*. New York: Citadel, 1963.

Schechter, Edmund, *Viennese Vignettes*. New York: Vantage, 1983.

Schuschnigg, Kurt von:
   Austrian Requiem. Transl. by Franz von Hildebrand. New York: G. P. Putnam's Sons, 1946.
   The Brutal Takeover. Transl. by Richard Barry. New York: Atheneum, 1971.

Seabury, Paul, *The Wilhelmstrasse*. Berkeley: Univ. of California Press, 1954.

Shirer, William L., *Berlin Diary*. New York: Alfred A. Knopf, 1941.

Shores, Christopher, *Duel for the Sky*. Garden City, N.Y.: Doubleday, 1985.

Snyder, Louis L., *Encyclopedia of the Third Reich*. New York: Paragon House, 1989.

Spiel, Hilde, *Vienna's Golden Autumn, 1866-1938*. New York: Weidenfeld and Nicolson, 1987.

Stein, George H., *The Waffen SS*. Ithaca, N.Y.: Cornell Univ. Press, 1966.

Tantum, W. H., and E. J. Hoffschmidt, eds., *The Rise and Fall of the German Air Force, 1933-1945*. Old Greenwich, Conn.: WE, 1969.

Taylor, Telford:
   Munich: The Price of Peace. Garden City, N.Y.: Doubleday, 1979.
   Sword and Swastika. New York: Simon and Schuster, 1952.

Thomson, S. Harrison, *Czechoslovakia in European History*. Princeton, N.J.: Princeton Univ. Press, 1943.

Toland, John, *Adolf Hitler*. New York: Ballantine Books, 1976.

Vital, David, "Czechoslovakia and the Powers, September 1938." In *European Diplomacy between Two Wars, 1919-1939*. Ed. by Hans W. Gatzke. Chicago: Quadrangle Books, 1972.

Völker, Karl-Heinz, *Die Deutsche Luftwaffe, 1933-1939*. Stuttgart: Deutsche Verlags-Anstalt, 1967.

Waites, Neville, ed., *Troubled Neighbours*. London: Weidenfeld and Nicolson, 1971.

Wallace, William V., *Czechoslovakia*. Boulder, Colo.: Westview, 1976.

Watt, Richard M., *Bitter Glory: Poland and Its Fate, 1918 to 1939*. New York: Simon and Schuster, 1979.

Weinberg, Gerhard L.:
   The Foreign Policy of Hitler's Germany: Diplomatic Revolution in Europe, 1933-1936. Chicago: Univ. of Chicago Press, 1970.
   The Foreign Policy of Hitler's Germany: Starting World War II, 1937-1939. Chicago: Univ. of Chicago Press, 1980.

Weingartner, James J., *Hitler's Guard: The Story of the Leibstandarte SS Adolf Hitler, 1933-1945*. Carbondale: Southern Illinois Univ. Press, 1968.

Wheeler-Bennett, John W., *Munich: Prologue to Tragedy*. New York: Duell, Sloan and Pearce, 1948.

Periodicals

Boeninger, Hildegard, "Hitler and the German Generals, 1934-1938." *Journal of Central European Affairs*, April 1954.

Cienciala, Anna M., "Poland and the Munich Crisis, 1938: A Reappraisal." *East European Quarterly*, June 1969.

Gunston, David, "Leni Riefenstahl." *Film*, fall 1960.

Mason, Tim, "The Workers' Opposition in Nazi Germany." *History Workshop Journal*, spring 1981.

Weinberg, Gerhard L.:
   "Hitler and England, 1933-1945: Pretense and Reality." *German Studies Review*, May 1985.
   "Munich after 50 Years." *Foreign Affairs*, fall 1988.

Ethnic Germans: in Poland, *142-143;* in the Ukraine, *17. See also* German Austrians; Germany; Sudeten Germans

Europe, central: *map* 14-15

F

Fatherland Front (Austrian party): 43, 55, 59

Fey, Emil: commander of Vienna Heimwehr, 56; and Vienna coup attempt, 56-57

Florence (Italy): *74, 76-77*

Foreign Ministry: dislike of Ribbentrop, 25; Hitler's rift with, 34

Four-Year Plan: Göring as director of, 34-35, 40; Luftwaffe favored in, 35; as preparation for war, 34; and synthetic materials, 34

France: and Czech crisis, 87-88, 91-92, 96-98; Czech dependence on, 85-86; depression's effect on, 27; as enemy of Germany, 38; fears German rearmament, 27; Hitler on, 38; Hitler's plans for, 14-16, 106, 168; and invasion of Poland, 156; issues ultimatum to Germany, 156; military strength of, 88-89; mobilizes for war (1938), 105; mutual-assistance pact with Soviet Union (1935), 21; pledges support to Greece and Rumania, 142; pledges support to Poland, 141-142, 147; and Polish crisis, 141-142, 144; prepares for war (1939), 144; relations with Germany, 34; and reoccupation of the Rhineland, 29-30. *See also* Allies

Franco, Francisco: 33

François-Poncet, André: and annexation of Sudetenland, 111; and Czech crisis, 100, 105, 106; on Göring, 107; on Ribbentrop, 25; warns against Germany, 30

Franz Ferdinand (archduke of Austria): assassination of, 46

French army: enters German territory, 164

Freud, Sigmund: and invasion of Austria, 68

Fritsch, Werner von: court-martial of, 41; death of, 166; and Hitler, 38-40; on Hitler, 40; homosexuality alleged, 40-41; at Hossbach conference (1937), 35-38; military cautiousness of, 40; resigns, 41

G

Gamelin, Maurice: and Polish defense plans, 146

Geneva Disarmament Conference: German participation in, 19-20; Germany withdraws from, 20; Weizsäcker on, 20

German Austrians: and Anschluss, 45, 51. *See also* Ethnic Germans; Germany

German diplomatic corps: anti-Semitism in, 19; Göring on, 19; Hitler on, 24

German Labor Front (DAF): Ley as head of, 18

German rearmament: 19, 21-26, 27; France fears, 27; Hitler announces, 21; Hitler on, 16; Pilsudsky and, 19

Germans, ethnic: *See* Ethnic Germans

Germany: *map* 14-15; alliance with Italy, 16, 35; annexes Czechoslovakia, 113; Austria becomes province of, 67; demands access through the Polish Corridor, 138, 140; demands return of Danzig, 137-138, 139, 140; food rationing introduced, 147; France as enemy of, 38; François-Poncet warns against, 30; Great Britain and France issue ultimatum to, 156; Great Britain as enemy of, 38; invades Poland, 124, *134;* involvement in Spanish Civil War, 33, 34; marches into Austria, 64-68, *66-67;* military strength of, 88-89; mobilizes for war (1938), 96, 99-100, 109; naval agreement with Great Britain (1935), 21-24, 25-26, 142; nonaggression pact with Poland, 20, 135, 138, 142, 149; nonaggression pact with Soviet Union, 146-147, 165; occupies Memel, 140-141; participates in Geneva Disarmament Conference, 19-20; propaganda attacks on Czechoslovakia, 86; relations with France, 34; relations with Japan, 31, 33; relations with Poland, 135-137, 147; relations with Soviet Union, 34; Saar votes for reunion with, 21, *22-23;* seizes Prague, *112-113;* treaty with Austria (1936), 33, 59; withdraws from Geneva Disarmament Conference, 20; withdraws from League of Nations, 20, 29. *See also* Ethnic Germans; German Austrians; Sudeten Germans

Goebbels, Joseph: and Czech crisis, 99, 100, 105; and reoccupation of the Rhineland, 29; on Ribbentrop, 24

Göring, Hermann: *35, 64, 113;* and Anschluss, 60-61, 64-65, 67; and Czech crisis, 99, 105; on Czechoslovakia, 86; on diplomatic corps, 19; as director of Four-Year Plan, 34-35, 40; François-Poncet on, 107; at Hossbach conference (1937), 35-38; as Luftwaffe commander, 34; on Luftwaffe in invasion of Poland, 168; at Munich conference (1938), *107;* plots against Blomberg, 40; plots against Fritsch, 40-41; on Poland, 137; and Revertera, 60-61; on Ribbentrop, 24

Great Britain: and Czech crisis, 87-89, 91-98; depression's effect on, 27; drops leaflets over the Rhineland, 164-165; as enemy of Germany, 38; and guilt over Treaty of Versailles, 27; Hitler on, 38; Hitler's plans for, 16, 106; and invasion of Poland, 156; issues ultimatum to Germany, 156; Japan as threat to, 27; military inadequacy of, 88-89; mobilizes for war (1938), 100, 105; naval agreement with Germany (1935), 21-24, 25-26, 142; pledges support to Greece and Rumania, 142; pledges support to Poland, 141-142, 147; and Polish crisis, 141-142, 144; relations with Germany, 34; and reoccupation of the Rhineland, 30; Ribbentrop as ambassador to, 31; Ribbentrop on, 31; Rosenberg on diplomatic mission to, 17-18, 24, 25. *See also* Allies

Great Powers: *See* Allies; France; Great Britain

Greece: Great Britain and France pledge support to, 142

Guderian, Heinz: 151, 162; on armored warfare, 161; fired on by German artillery, 154; tours Polish battlefield, 156-161

H

Habicht, Theodor: in German embassy in Vienna, 18

Habsburgs: dynasty collapses, 46; and Protestant Reformation, 45; as rulers of Austria, 44-45

Hácha, Emil: meets with Hitler, 113; as president of Czechoslovakia, 112-113

Halifax, Lord: and Czech crisis, 89

Hammerstein-Equord, Kurt von: 13, 16

Heimwehr: 52-53, 54, 55, 59; battle with Schutzbund, 56; Fey as commander in Vienna, 56; in Vienna coup attempt, 57-58, *60-61*

Hel Peninsula: siege of, 155, 163, 168

Henderson, Sir Nevile: 89; and Czech crisis, 105; on Hitler, 142; and Polish crisis, 147

Henkell, Otto: 24

Henlein, Konrad: *88;* Ashton-Gwatkin on, 92; and formation of Sudeten German party, 85; Hitler supports, 86-87, 89; incites Czech government, 86-87, 89, 91-96; Runciman and, 91-92

Himmler, Heinrich: and invasion of Austria, 64, 68

Hindenburg Group: *See* Luftwaffe: Kampfgeschwader 1

Hindenburg, Paul von: 38; and Neurath, 17, 18

Hitler, Adolf: abandons plans to invade Czechoslovakia, 100-105; addresses the Reichstag (1939), 142; admires Mussolini, 16, 31; and Anglo-German Naval Agreement (1935), *26;* and anti-Semitism, 14, 143; assumes command of armed forces, 41; on Austria, 44, 45; and Austrian Catholics, 72; Blomberg and, 38-40; as chancellor, 13; and concept of master race, 14; controls Brauchitsch, 41; on Czech defense plans, 93; Daladier on, 106; on diplomatic corps, 24; diplomatic skills, 26; expansionist policies of, 13-16, 35-38; fiftieth birthday celebration, *4-11;* on France, 38; friendship with Ribbentrop, 24-26; Fritsch and, 38-40; Fritsch on, 40; on German rearmament, 16; on Great Britain, 38; Henderson on, 142; at Hossbach conference (1937), 35-38; intimidates Schuschnigg, 62-64, 139; introduces conscription, 21; on Italy, 74, 75; in Landsberg prison, 14; on lebensraum, 13, 35-38; meets with Beck, 139, *140;* meets with Chamberlain, 92-97, 99; meets with Ciano (1936), 33; meets with Hácha, 113; meets with Mussolini (1934), 33;

Time-Life Books Inc. offers a wide range of fine recordings, including a Rock 'n' Roll Era series. For subscription information, call 1-800-621-7026 or write Time-Life Music, P.O. Box C-32068, Richmond, Virginia 23261-2068.